Great Stories of the Victoria Cross

Great Stories of the Victoria Cross

Brigadier The Rt Hon Sir John Smyth, Bt, VC, MC

ARTHUR BARKER LIMITED LONDON
A subsidiary of Weidenfeld (Publishers) Limited

Photoset by Weatherby Woolnough,
Wellingborough, Northants
Printed in Great Britain by
Morrison & Gibb Ltd, London and Edinburgh

Please renew/return this item by the last date shown.

So that your telephone call is charged at local rate, please call the numbers as set out below:

	From Area codes 01923 or 0208:	From the rest of Herts:
Renewals:	01923 471373	01438 737373
Enquiries:	01923 471333	01438 737333
Minicom:	01923 471599	01438 737599

L32b

Money lost – little lost
Honour lost – much lost
Courage lost – all lost
Courage is the thing

This book is dedicated
With kind permission
To our beloved Sovereign

THE QUEEN

Who throughout her reign
Has taken the closest interest in
The Victoria Cross
Particularly during the last twenty years
When she has been the Gracious Patron of
The Victoria Cross and George Cross Association

Contents

Illustrations

Foreword

There is no doubt that, as the years go by and the living holders of the Victoria Cross decrease in numbers, public interest in our premier decoration for bravery in battle becomes greater. In 1975 a Victoria Cross fetched nearly £8000 in an auction in London, and vc memorials have been established in Britain, Australia and Canada. The fact that the Queen and Prince Philip should have given a reception at Windsor Castle for the members of the Victoria Cross and George Cross Association on 21 April, Her Majesty's fiftieth birthday, stimulated even greater interest in these two famous decorations.

I am particulalry struck by the number of young people who write to me about the Victoria Cross and who have made a study of the subject; they are interested not merely in the actual act which won the Cross but in the circumstances which surrounded it.

Many people ask me what sort of men win the Victoria Cross. I can only reply, any sort. Courage is a queer thing which we all have in a greater or lesser degree and men react to different stresses and dangers in different ways. And there are many sorts of courage. In this book, of course, I am only dealing with courage in battle. For most people I believe that courage is expendable. This alone makes it very difficult to predict. Some of the holders of the Victoria Cross that I have known have appeared to be without fear – such people as General Carton de Wiart, Lord Freyberg, Lord Gort and Group Captain Leonard Cheshire. But only they can say whether this is really so. Most people are afraid of something, most of us of many things. How lucky are those whose courage is high at the important moment – and when someone is looking. I have occasionally seen some unknown man do something incredibly brave in battle – and then been completely obliterated by a shell burst – as though he had never been.

There is, I think, one characteristic of all vc incidents. Those who have won the Cross have all – on that particular occasion at any rate – been prepared to sacrifice their lives; the number of posthumous vcs in itself seems to bear this out. His life is the most precious thing a man can offer – and life is most precious to young people, such as most of those who have won the Victoria Cross. If there is one single common denominator amongst vcs I would be inclined to say that it is a degree of obstinacy – a refusal to be beaten or pushed around. And if there is one quality which almost all those vcs I have known are totally deficient in, it is conceit. Although they are naturally – and very rightly – proud of the highest of all decorations they wear, they never cease to remember that there were many others who have possibly deserved it as much or more than they have.

I am very proud to have known so many of these charming and gallant people and to have been, for all the twenty years it has existed, either Chairman or President of their Association. When my publishers asked me to write this particular book of old heroisms retold, I was honoured and delighted to do so. The stories I have described are not necessarily the *greatest* stories of the vc – comparisons are odious and, besides, in one short book only a very limited number can be included. But they are stories 'across the board' of the century and more of the life of the Victoria Cross. I hope that my readers, like Oliver Twist, will ask for more.

Jackie Smyth

Acknowledgements

My warmest thanks are due to my publishers who invited me to write this book and have co-operated so enthusiastically in its production; to Her Majesty the Queen who has so graciously agreed to my dedicating the book to her; to the Ministry of Defence Librarian and the Imperial War Museum and National Army Museum for their ever ready help over books and photos; to those many VCs whom I have been privileged to know over the last half century of my life; and to my wife Frances who has given such valuable support to the VC and GC Association and has typed and sub-edited this book as well as all the thirty others I have written.

Jackie Smyth

Introduction

When Queen Victoria instituted this greatest of all awards for gallantry on the field of battle in 1856 – and later made it retrospective to the autumn of 1854 to cover the period of the Crimean War – she 'expressly desired that the new decoration should be highly prized and eagerly sought after'. Prince Edward of Wales, later King Edward VIII, presiding at the VC dinner which he had arranged in the royal gallery of the House of Lords in 1929, described the VC as 'The most democratic and at the same time the most exclusive of all orders of chivalry – the most enviable order of the Victoria Cross.' After a passage of a hundred and twenty years, it is generally considered to be the greatest decoration for courage in battle of all time.

The Cross consists of a Maltese Cross of bronze made from the metal of one of the Russian guns captured at Sebastopol, with the royal crest in the centre and underneath a scroll bearing the words 'For Valour'. On the reverse side of the Cross is the date of the act of bravery, whilst the name of the recipient is engraved at the back of the clasp. At first the ribbon was blue for the Navy and red for the Army. But, by the royal warrant of 22 May 1920, signed by the then Secretary of State for War, Winston Churchill, the ribbon is red for all the Services and when the ribbon only is worn a small replica of the Cross is fixed in the centre.

In the case of conspicuous bravery on the part of a body of sailors or soldiers (and later of airmen), officers and other ranks had the privilege of selecting one or more of their number for the honour. In earlier wars – particularly in the Indian Mutiny – a number of awards to a unit were decided in this way. Later the practice died out almost completely. A bar could be awarded for a further act of supreme courage and three such bars have been won.

Four civilians have been awarded the Victoria Cross: three were magistrates of the Bengal Civil Service in the Indian Mutiny, and the fourth was to a Bengal clergyman who won it in the Afghan War. Civilians are still eligible for the VC if serving with the armed forces. Members of the Womens' Services are eligible for the award, but up to date no woman has won it. The American Unknown Soldier was awarded the Victoria Cross.

The total number of awards of the Victoria Cross is 1,351, exclusive of the American Unknown Soldier. Between 1854 and 1 August 1914, 522 VCs were awarded. These included 112 in the Crimea and 182 in the Indian Mutiny. Between 2 August 1914 and 30 April 1920, the period of the First World War, there were 633 awards. Between 1 May 1920 and December 1938 there were five. In the Second World War there were 182 and since then there have been nine. These latter comprise four in Korea (1950–51), one to a Gurkha in Sarawak (1965) and four to Australians in Vietnam (1965-69). There have been 1,348 actual recipients of the Victoria Cross as three of them were double VCs. At our tenth Victoria Cross and George Cross reunion in London in April 1976 there were only 117 VCs still living.

It will be noted that the number of awards of the VC in the Indian Mutiny was exactly the same as that in the Second World War. It must be remembered, however, that in the earlier wars, before the First and Second World Wars of 1914-18 and 1939-45, the VC and DCM were virtually the only decorations which could be won for gallantry on the field of battle. Later on there were the DSO, MC, MM, DSC, DSM, DFC and IDSM. Had these decorations existed at the time of the Mutiny and the Crimea, for instance, they would undoubtedly have been awarded in many cases instead of the VC. It will also be noted that by far the largest number of awards of the VC were made in the First World War of 1914-18, where the grim, close-quarter trench-warfare fighting and the very heavy casualties resulted in so many VC incidents.

The largest number of VCs awarded to one regiment in an action is seven – to the South Wales Borderers at Rorke's Drift in the Zulu War of 1879. In the Gallipoli landings in 1915 the Lancashire Fusiliers won 'six VCs before breakfast'.

In general, the VC is naturally a young man's award; but there are a number of exceptions. The oldest man ever to receive the VC was Lieutenant (later Captain) William Raynor, who was a member of the Bengal Veteran Establishment. He won his VC at the Delhi magazine in the Indian Mutiny on 11 May 1857 and is believed to have been sixty-nine at the time. Eighteen VCs have been known to have been under twenty: two of the youngest recorded were Hospital Apprentice Andrew Fitzgibbon of the Indian Medical Estalishment (Taku Forts, China, 21 August 1860), who was just over fifteen ; and Boy J. T. Cornwell (Jutland, 31 May 1916) aged sixteen. But there may be several more, as some VCs tended to give the wrong age so as to be enlisted and, particularly in the Indian Army, the date of birth was not always known.

In 1956, the centenary year of the Victoria Cross, at the request of a number of my fellow VCs attending the reunion of that year, the suggestion of some national newspapers and of the President of the Royal Society of St George, I founded the Victoria Cross Association (which afterwards became the Victoria Cross and George Cross Association). It had been twenty-seven years since the last VC reunion in London and the holders felt that there should be an Association which would keep them in touch with one another and allow them all to meet in London at more frequent intervals.

I had just completed two ministerial appointments in the Ministry of Pensions and in the Ministry of Pensions and National Insurance, which had kept me in close contact with the ex-Service Associations and the military hospitals. I lived in London and had an office there so that I was a convenient choice.

The young Association got off to a good start and we were very thrilled when Her Majesty the Queen honoured us by becoming our Patron and Sir Winston Churchill agreed to become our first Life President. I remained Chairman for fifteen years and was elected to succeed him as President on his death. I was succeeded as Chairman by Rear-Admiral Godfrey Place, VC.

Since then, starting in 1958, the members of the VC and GC Association have met in London every two years. At our first reunion Mr Duncan Sandys (now Lord Duncan Sandys), then Minister of Defence, gave us a pledge that members of the Association would never be prevented from attending our reunions by any difficulties of transport or finance. This pledge has been honoured by successive British Governments, and the RAF and the Canadian and Australian Air Forces have been most helpful in bringing our members over from the Commonwealth.

The Queen and Prince Philip have given splendid receptions for us in Buckingham Palace and at Windsor Castle and many members of the royal family, prime ministers and distinguished people, have honoured us by their presence at our gatherings.

As the Prince of Wales said so many years ago, the Victoria Cross is the most *democratic* of all the orders of chivalry. In the words of Kipling:

> There is neither East nor West
> Border nor breed nor birth
> When two strong men stand face to face
> Though they come from the ends of the earth.

This has been the aim of the Association since its foundation.

I am indeed honoured to have been so closely connected with so many gallant men, who are naturally proud of their high decoration, but always humble in the knowledge that many others deserved it as much or more than they did. Our numbers decrease sadly each year but the monument of the Victoria Cross lives on in the memorials set up in London and in the British Commonwealth – and in the hearts of the British people.

Lord Carew, Chairman of the British Legion, once wrote to me as Chairman of the Association: 'There is no doubt that you have forged yet another of those intangible but most effective links of gossamer which are yet as steel, holding us all together in a changing world.'

1

The Charge of
the Light Brigade.

Cannon to right of them, cannon to left of them,
Cannon in front of them volleyed and thundered
When can their glory fade, O the wild charge they made
All the world wondered.

Alfred, Lord Tennyson.

It was at Balaclava on 25 October 1854, on the bleak plateau above Sebastopol that the cavalry action took place which passed into history as 'The Charge of the Light Brigade'. The British people have seldom been so stirred by any episode in their history. Books and articles have been written about it, films have been made of it, but nothing gave it so much publicity as Lord Tennyson's famous poem. And yet – vivid and terrific as the story is – the famous charge was the result of a combination of human failings, tactical errors and crass stupidity almost past belief. Only the courage of the men and the horses are beyond praise. And what a terrible massacre of noble horseflesh it was ! It was difficult enough to tend to the wounded – the sufferings of the mangled horses is too horrible to contemplate.

Forty years of peace had resulted in a considerable deterioration in the command structure of the Army. Many of the senior officers were too old for active command in the field and others were lacking in experience and knowledge, largely owing to the system of purchase of promotion and command. The cavalry had become wedded to charging in serried ranks rather than in undertaking any form of flexible manoeuvre. The system of communicating orders in the field was prehistoric, as was evidenced in the famous charge. The rank and file were well disciplined and well led in respect of their unit commanders and their courage and endurance were remarkable. Flogging was, of course, still the chief punishment for serious offences but was seldom resorted to in good regiments.

On the morning of this historic action the cavalry brigades, the Light and the Heavy, stood to their horses an hour before dawn. As the sun rose Lord Lucan, commanding the Cavalry Division, rode forward with his staff. Lord Cardigan, who commanded the Light Brigade, had not yet joined from his yacht in Balaclava harbour, where he went back to sleep each night. What a way to command troops in battle, and what a terrible example to set to all his subordinates!

In the half light of the early morning it became apparent that à large force of Russians was advancing, with a mass of cavalry in support. There is no doubt that the British, with no outposts or piquets in position, were taken completely by surprise. As the Russians approached to within 400 yards Lord Lucan ordered Brigadier Scarlett, who commanded the Heavy Brigade, to attack. The Greys, the Inniskillings and the 4th Dragoon Guards flung themselves upon the massed Russian cavalry and hurled them back. In eight pulsating minutes the Heavies, effectively supported by the 93rd Highlanders, had driven four times their number from the field for the loss of only seventy-eight killed and wounded.

This brilliant exploit, however, was entirely eclipsed in the popular memory by the heroic but catastrophic charge of the Light Brigade, which should never have taken place and achieved nothing except to demonstrate the do-or-die spirit of the British soldier.

The Commander-in-Chief, Lord Raglan, sent the following message to Lord Lucan: 'Cavalry to advance and take advantage of any opportunity to recover the heights.' A little later on, having been told by his staff that a party of Russians were about to withdraw, taking with them their captured Turkish guns, Lord Raglan sent another order to Lord Lucan, telling him that he wished the cavalry to advance rapidly to prevent this operation. Captain Nolan, an officer of the 15th Hussars, who was one of the up-and-coming staff-trained intellectuals of the Army – and as such was anathema to Lord Lucan – carried this message. In his full dress cavalry uniform he presented a gallant and colourful figure as he galloped up to the divisional commander. But by the time he arrived the situation had changed and the order meant nothing to Lord Lucan.

However, it was marked 'immediate' and its urgency was emphasized by the whole excited demeanour of Captain Nolan. When Lord Lucan queried the order Captain Nolan replied, pointing vaguely down the valley: 'There my Lord is your enemy ! There are your guns !'

Lord Lucan, irritated and indignant beyond measure at what seemed to him to be a taunt at his own courage, made no further attempt to clarify the meaning of the order but rode over to Lord Cardigan and gave him an order which the latter understood was to charge the long line of Russian guns some 2000 yards distant at the end of the valley. This was a classic example of a vague order, badly delivered, and improperly interpreted, leading to the death of many fine and gallant men, for Lord Cardigan, though he shared Lord Lucan's misgivings, immediately ordered the Light Brigade to advance down the valley.

The first line of the Brigade consisted of the 17th Lancers and the 13th Light Dragoons. The second line, led by Lord George Paget, consisted of the 11th Hussars, the 4th Light Dragoons and the 8th Hussars. The brigade maintained its direction straight down the valley, shelled by the Russian guns on the heights to its left, the captured guns on the right and the guns at the head of the valley, as well as being fired on by large numbers of Russian rifleman, pushed down to the foot of the slopes. No wonder the French general, Bosquet, gave vent to that famous and much-quoted remark : '*C'est magnifique, mais ce n'est pas la guerre.*'

This ill-starred but most heroic charge became a legend of British history. The Light Brigade, despite suffering heavily, reached its objective, cut down those Russian gunners who still remained at their posts, and even charged into the Russian cavalry beyond. The survivors came back, battered, wounded, weary, exalted, many of them walking and leaving their dead, or wounded horses behind ; but when these first feelings had worn off, disillusioned and despondent.

No one will ever know all the deeds of valour that were performed in that ghastly, hell-torn valley of screaming horses and tortured human flesh. But somehow this very gallant action against hopeless odds was a fit mid-wife to the birth of the Victoria Cross.

The nine Balaclava Victoria Crosses were : Sergeant-Major John Berryman, Sergeant John Farrell, and Sergeant-Major Charles Wooden, 17th Lancers ; Sergeant-Major John Grieve and Sergeant Henry Ramage, 2nd Dragoons (Scots Greys); Lieutenant Alexander Robert Dunn, 11th Hussars ; Private Samuel Parkes, 4th Hussars ; Sergeant Joseph Malone, 13th Light Dragoons ; Surgeon James Mouat, 6th Dragoons.

2

The Indian Mutiny.

In May 1857, in the middle of the hot weather, the Indian Mutiny started and a small British garrison of some 28,000 troops, together with the British officers of the Native Army, the loyal element of that army and the British families and civilians, had to sustain an ordeal of unparalleled drama, danger, anxiety and hardship. For a time it looked as though India might be lost to Britain with all the tragic consequences that would have entailed.

Field-Marshal Lord Wolseley, who had been recommended for the Victoria Cross as a junior officer in the Crimea, and who later served in the Indian Mutiny, wrote :

The Indian Mutiny abounded in examples of British heroism, of which our race has very reason to be proud. It was a period of storm and stress, of honour and glory. Its history abounds in military events of transcendent national importance. The self-sacrifice in the cause of country and in the maintenance of our wide empire, which fills the history of the Mutiny, should be learnt by every British schoolboy.

This somewhat eulogistic statement did in fact convey quite accurately what it was like. No less than 182 VCs were awarded in the Mutiny campaign.

No one should imagine that the Mutiny was just a conflict of black against white. It would have gone hard with the British if a considerable part of the Native Army had not remained loyal. Whole races, such as the martial Sikhs and Gurkhas, remained absolutely loyal to the British and rendered inestimable service. Even in the regiments which mutinied there were many cases of sepoys who did their best to protect their British officers at the risk of their own lives.

The story of the Mutiny is not a pleasant one. The constant anxiety of the British was for the safety of their women and children, and the brutal killing of civilians in the early days roused the British troops to white hot feelings of revenge which sometimes resulted in horrible retaliation; and of course mutiny was an offence punishable by death. There were deeds of great gallantry on both sides; and on the part of British women, in conditions of appalling heat and danger, there was almost unbelievable heroism.

A great deal has been written about the Mutiny. In this chapter I shall describe only the first VCs awarded for the defence of the Delhi magazine on 11 May 1857, the day after the Mutiny had started in Meerut; and the gallant defence of Lucknow, which was an epic in British history, and attracted sixty VCs.

In contrast to Meerut, with its strong British contingent, Delhi was garrisoned entirely by native troops. The large and very important magazine at Delhi was in the city. It contained two complete siege trains, brand new field guns, shells, powder, rifles and vast quantities of cartridges. It was in the charge of Lieutenant George Willoughby of the Bengal Artillery, with eight British assistants, all middle-aged men, and a large native establishment.

Monday, 11 May was just another hot day to Lieutenant Willoughby. No news of the Meerut mutiny had reached him, from where the Native Army mutineers, after murdering most of their British officers and a certain number of their wives, had set fire to their own lines and disappeared in the direction of Delhi. But very soon eyewitness reports reached Willoughby and a short time later he saw the Meerut mutineers streaming across the river and entering the city by the Palace Gate.

Lieutenant Willoughby, a quiet, steadfast type of man, realized at once that the magazine would be the first objective, not only of the mutineers, but of all the riff-raff elements of the city. He imagined quite naturally that the British units of the Meerut garrison would soon be coming to his aid – and no one has really been able to explain why they never did.

It was soon evident that the native element in the magazine were not to be trusted and the nine Englishmen prepared to fight to the last and, if necessary, to blow up the magazine rather than let it fall into the hands of the mutineers. The outer gates were closed and barricaded and the guns were brought out, placed in position and loaded with grape. Then a train of gunpowder was laid from the powder magazine so that, if further defence appeared hopeless, the magazine could be blown.

Soon the Meerut mutineers were swarming over the walls of the magazine by means of scaling ladders and they were joined by the native element of the garrison. Lieutenant Willoughby let them go as there was nothing he could do to stop them. Then the mutineers opened a murderous fire from the tops of the walls, to which the nine valiant Englishmen replied with guns and rifles. There could be only one end to this unequal encounter. At all costs the magazine had to be blown before too many of the small band of defenders were put out of action. This was the moment of decision and perhaps the bravest one of the whole of the Indian Mutiny operations.

Conductor Buckley, who was to give the signal, had already been wounded. Willoughby therefore gave the signal himself and Conductor Scully fired the train. At about 4 pm, with a terrific roar which shook the whole of Delhi, the great magazine exploded.

Not one of the defenders expected to escape with his life but Willoughby, Buckley, Forrest and Raynor, so smoke blackened that they looked more black than white, managed to get away. The three latter, Buckley and Forrest being badly wounded, managed to reach Meerut safely but the gallant Willoughby became separated from them and was killed. The three survivors were awarded the vc. Raynor, who was believed to be sixty-nine at the time, was the oldest man ever to receive the Cross.

I have often wondered how Raynor managed to escape with his life so that I was most interested to receive a letter from a former brother officer regarding the story of the Delhi Magazine, and I quote from it as follows:

I wonder if you ever met Cyril Raynor or heard him talk about his grandfather's vc? According to his story, as far as I can remember after a great many years, at the time of the blowing up of the arsenal at Delhi the older Raynor and his wife and infant son were standing under one of the two stone entrances to the arsenal which, as you know, were not seriously damaged. (In fact you must have seen them often, still standing in the middle of the road leading from the Kashmir Gate to the front of the Red Fort).

An enormous and hostile crowd was approaching the arsenal with the intention of capturing it and looting it but broke up and fled when the explosion occurred – all except one, an Akali Sikh of frightening appearance in his black robe with his kirpan at his side, who showed no fear and continued to advance slowly but determinedly. He was more than friendly and escorted the Raynors through byways to the river bank, accompanied them in a boat across the Jumna and led them to a Jat village where they were well looked after . . . Cyril said that when he was a small boy he used to see the then very old Akali who used to call on his father once a year to receive the pension which Raynor gave him.

The next three Victoria Crosses were won at Benares on the night of 4 June. Sergeant-Major M. Rosamond of the 37th Bengal Native Infantry, Sergeant-Major Peter Gill of the Ludhiana Regiment (later 15th Ludhiana Sikhs) and Private John Kirk of the 10th Foot (the Lincolnshire Regiment), volunteered to save British personnel and their wives and children when their lives were threatened by the mutineers of the 25th and 37th Regiments of Bengal Native Infantry. Sergeant-Major Gill also twice saved the life of Major Barrett of the 27th Regiment when that officer was attacked by Sepoys of his own regiment.

Meanwhile in Delhi the most terrible atrocities were taking place and very few of the Europeans, Eurasians or Indian Christians who happened to be in the city escaped from the frenzy of the mutineers and the mob. Then followed the siege and finally the assault and capture of Delhi, which was a great VC story in itself and a turning point in the Mutiny for which sixteen VCs were awarded. Although the main crisis of the Mutiny centred round Delhi, the epic story of the whole campaign was that of Lucknow.

Lucknow was the capital of Oudh, the Governor of which province was Sir Henry Lawrence, one of the greatest administrators India has ever known. He had at his disposal one British regiment, the 32nd Foot (The Duke of Cornwall's Light Infantry), and four native units, one cavalry and three infantry. His first problem was whether or not to try to disarm the Indian troops. He decided not to do so and thereby, in the light of after events, probably made a mistake. He realized perfectly well that a grave crisis was impending and he at once set about preparing the Residency for a last ditch resistance.

The Residency building, by itself, was too small to hold all the men, women and children who would have to be accommodated there. An enclosure, therefore, was marked out around it, the perimeter of which consisted of small buildings, linked together by an earthwork. Portions of the perimeter were overlooked by high buildings which should have been demolished, but as the tallest of them were mosques or temples they were left alone. It was traditionally the British way not to interfere with religion, but they were to prove a great menace throughout the siege and caused the garrison many casualties.

The siege of Lucknow consisted of two phases, with a break of only a few hours between them. The first siege that the original small British community sustained – about 800 in all, including over 500 women and children – was from 30 June 1857 to 25 September and was the really heroic one. The ordeal which the garrison had to suffer grew worse with every day that passed. The Residency building was far from being shell-proof and on 2 July, the second day of the siege, Lawrence was mortally wounded by a shell which crashed through the wall of his bedroom.

As the siege continued the fighting strength of the garrison was reduced by battle casualties and by sickness. During the later weeks every fit man had to remain on duty permanently, as did also many of the sick and wounded. The ordeal of the women was terrible and the male survivors could only wonder in amazement at their fortitude and calmness. They appeared to fear neither wounds nor death and they played a valuable part in the routine of the defence. Their chief tribulation was the suffering and death of their children.

At last news was received of General Havelock's relieving column and in the late afternoon of 22 September the rumble of guns was heard. Hopes began to rise – and by the next day there was no shadow of doubt. The sound of musketry became sustained, the skirl of bagpipes could be faintly heard and through the flame and smoke of burning houses the garrison could see the kilts of the 78th Regiment (The Seaforth Highlanders) – who won five VCs at Lucknow – advancing. Within an hour they had broken through to the Residency – on 28 September – and at once they themselves became besieged. The second siege continued until 17 November, a further period of fifty-three days. It seemed almost incredible that such a flimsy little defence enclosure could have sustained such a persistent attack for so long. During the two sieges of Lucknow and the relief operations sixty VCs were won.

Throughout both sieges the British flag was kept flying over the Residency. The flagstaff was shattered many times but the garrison always managed to rig up another and the moral effect of seeing it there day after day was almost worth the sacrifice in lives entailed.

Towards the end of June 1947, only a few weeks before the transfer of power from British to Indian and Pakistani rule, it was decided that this shot-torn British flag which still flew over the Residency at Lucknow, should be hauled down at a suitable ceremony, but one that was necessarily subdued so as not to cause any political repercussions. As the Rajput Regiment, which had taken a prominent part in the defence of Lucknow, had its training centre nearby it seemed fitting that the regiment and a British regiment should parade for the occasion. In the end, however, to avoid the possibility of any disturbance, on the late evening of 13 August 1947, two days before the transfer of power, a small party of British officers went to the Residency and watched the Warrant officer in Charge haul down the flag. The flagstaff and its base were demolished during the night by British Sappers and the flag was sent to the Commander-in-Chief, Field-Marshal Sir Claude Auchinleck. At King George VI's request it was presented to him so that it could hang at Windsor Castle alongside other historic flags.

3

The Taking of the Taku Forts in the Third China War.

The origin of what was known as the Third China War was that the Chinese Government refused to admit the British and French envoys who went to Peking to ratify the treaty drawn up in the previous year. Although the Chinese had agreed to this on paper they never meant it to happen. When the British admiral, with several gun-boats, attempted to sail up the Pei-ho river *en route* for Peking, they were fired on by the Taku forts at the mouth of the river. The admiral then landed a considerable force of marines and bluejackets, which was repulsed with heavy loss. An expedition under General Sir James Hope Grant was therefore despatched to obtain satisfaction.

The expedition was an allied one, the French supplying a force of 7000 men, under General Montauban, and the British 11,000 under Sir James Hope Grant. The expedition, which assembled in Hong Kong, was faced with considerable transport difficulties, both sea and land, and would have been in dire straits without the Coolie Corps which was enlisted in Hong Kong. The Coolie Corps rendered first-rate service throughout the campaign : they were strong, plucky, cheerful and easy to manage and it was reckoned that one coolie was worth three baggage animals.

On 26 July 1860 the force embarked and reached the shallow waters of the Pei-ho river two days later. Next morning the allied force moved forward and took possession of Pehtang. They found the greatest difficulty in getting the guns through the marshy ground which had been made more soggy by recent rains. Sir James Hope Grant was determined not to attack the heavily defended Taku forts, which had

11

proved such a difficult proposition the previous year, until he could subject them to a severe artillery bombardment.

The advance infantry had suffered an unexpected mounted attack by a large body of Tartar cavalry, wearing cuirasses of gilded leather or chain mail, and long furred black boots. The infantry formed square to receive them as, mounted on ponies with high wooden saddles, they galloped furiously forward with their lances poised. They were caught by the British cavalry, King's Dragoon Guards and Sikhs, who charged into the thick of them and flung them back. Major D. M. Probyn, vc (later Sir Dighton), who led his Indian Cavalry Regiment, had won his vc in the Indian Mutiny.

The principal strength of the forts in resisting an attack from the landward side was the difficulty of the approach over mud-flats and numerous water-courses, necessitating the construction of many bridges and, in the later stages, the laying of pontoon bridges. By the night of 20 August everything was ready for the attack on the northern fort, which Sir James Hope Grant had rightly considered was the key to the whole Chinese position.

The artillery bombardment opened at 5 am on the twenty-first with eight heavy guns and three 8-inch mortars, two of the new Armstrong 12-pounder batteries, two 9-pounder batteries and one rocket battery. The enemy answered with all the guns they could bring to bear, amongst which were the two naval 32-pounders they had captured from the British the previous year. At 7 am the infantry attack started. A French battalion and two British battalions, the 44th Essex Regiment and the 67th Hampshire Regiment, were in the van. They vied with one another to be first into the fort.

Many of the stormers did not wait for the engineers with the pontoon bridges but plunged into the water and clambered up the other side. In some cases the men had to swim. The Chinese manned the walls with great determination and showered down on the attackers every sort of missile, from buckets of lime to 'stink-pots' and roundshot.

While the British endeavoured to scale the walls by standing on one another's shoulders the French had coolies bringing up scaling ladders. Lieutenant Robert Montresor Rogers of the 44th Essex Regiment was up on the walls first, closely supported by Private John McDougall of his own regiment, and Lieutenant Edmund Henry Lenon of the 67th

Hampshire Regiment. Lieutenant Nathaniel Burslem and Private Thomas Lane, also of the 67th, both of whom were seriously wounded, were hard on their heels and at once set to work to make a breach in the wall. Ensign John Worthy Chaplin was carrying the Queen's Colour of the 67th and first planted it on the breach made by the storming party, assisted by Private Lane. Chaplin then planted the Colour on the bastion of the fort, which he was the first to mount, but in so doing he was severely wounded. All these six men were awarded the Victoria Cross.

Hospital Apprentice Andrew FitzGibbon of the Indian Medical Service, who was attached to the 67th, also won the VC for his great courage and composure in attending to the wounded under heavy fire. He was severely wounded in the attempt. He was born on 13 May 1845 and was thus only fifteen years and three months old when he won his Cross. This is the youngest VC ever recorded.

Preparations were quickly made to take the second and larger fort ; but the Chinese had become disheartened at the loss of their main bastion and surrendered the fort without a fight. After some further show of resistance by parties of cavalry Tientsin was taken without a shot being fired towards the end of September.

Lord Elgin then arrived and started peace negotiations with the Emperor's Ambassador in Tientsin. Once again, however, the Chinese dragged their feet and Sir James Hope Grant was compelled to advance on Peking on 13 October and eventually to burn down the Summer Palace to bring the Chinese to their senses. All the British terms were then accepted without demur. So ended the China War of 1860.

13

4

The Zulu War.
Isandhlwana and the Heroic
Defence of Rorke's Drift.

Few campaigns have aroused so much public interest, and also so much controversy, as the Zulu War of 1879 which will always be remembered for the disaster at Isandhlwana and the heroic defence of Rorke's Drift, which won for the 24th Regiment (The South Wales Borderers) seven vcs, the largest number awarded to a regiment in one action.

Zululand was a territory bordering on the South African colony of Natal, from which it was separated by the Buffalo and Tugela rivers. The Zulus were the most formidable warriors in South Africa; their men were of fine physique and their military efficiency and discipline had been built up by a former chief who had fought against the British in 1799 and copied their methods. Their procedure in battle was swift and ruthless attack with the object of getting to close quarters as quickly as possible. They exploited that greatest of all principles of war, surprise, by the secrecy of their approach to their objective and the great speed with which they carried out their plan of attack. Their tactics were apt to be alarming to young and unseasoned troops as the British discovered to their cost. A number of Zulus were armed with rifles but their main weapon was the assegai, first used by throwing and then, at close quarters, by stabbing. They would advance courageously through a hail of bullets to close with their enemy.

At the time the Zulu campaign opened the Zulus were ruled by King Cetywayo, an arrogant and aggressive character. Finally a British force was sent to deal with him in January 1879 under command of Lord Chelmsford. The Isandhlwana disaster occurred when the defended camp Lord Chelmsford had left at that place, as he moved out with the main body of his column, was overrun in broad daylight by a surprise

14

attack of a large force of Zulus. The garrison left behind in Isandhlwana camp consisted of a small mixed force of Regulars, Colonists and Native Levies, under temporary command of Brevet-Lieutenant Colonel Pulleine of the 1/24th Regiment. The Regulars consisted of five companies of the 1/24th, one company of the 2/24th; seventy-two men of N Battery, Royal Horse Artillery with two guns; thirty mounted infantry; fifty-five mounted Volunteers; thirty-three Natal Mounted Police; four companies Natal Native Contingent and eleven Natal Native Pioneers. All told, including camp followers, they numbered about 1,330, of whom about 800 were Europeans.

The defensive position had been selected by Lord Chelmsford himself. It consisted of an isolated flat-topped hill, under 300 yards in length with precipitous sides along its whole perimeter. The ground in front of the camp, and to the sides, fell away from the hill in an easy slope, perfectly open for a distance of at least 800 yards. Lord Chelmsford said afterwards: 'I consider that there never was a position where a small force could have made a better defensive stand.'

How was it then that in broad daylight the camp was overrun by a force of Zulus who relied almost entirely on a massed attack with the assegai ? There were, of course, certain weaknesses in the Isandhlwana defence, the chief of which was perhaps that the Native Levies were of doubtful quality. There was no trench round the perimeter, the ground being too rocky, but a trench, though a protection against rifle fire, would have been of no avail against a rush of Zulus. The concentrated fire of the companies of the South Wales Borderers should have been more than sufficient to repel any Zulu attack on the camp perimeter. The trouble was they were not there when the attack took place. Colonel Pulleine had received written orders to draw in his camp defences as well as his outpost line, but to keep his mounted vedettes well out in advance.

At 8 am on the morning of the twenty-second the vedettes reported a body of Zulus advancing towards the camp and Colonel Pulleine ordered the troops to stand to arms. So far so good. At 10 am Colonel Durnford arrived with welcome reinforcements of some South Wales Borderers from Rorke's Drift and assumed command from Colonel Pulleine in accordance with Lord Chelmsford's instructions. All was quiet at the camp. Colonel Durnford, however, seemed to have quite a different idea of his task as camp commander from Colonel Pulleine. He seemed to think that he should assume a much more offensive role and he accordingly moved out of the camp with a number of Basutos and Native Levies and ordered one company of the 1/24th, under Lieutenant Cavaye, to take up a position on some high ground about 1,500 yards north of the camp.

Colonel Pulleine felt bound to protest against this departure from the orders he had received from Lord Chelmsford, but he eventually bowed to the ruling of his superior officer.

At noon everything was quiet in the camp and the troops were sent to their tents for dinner. Suddenly, however, reports began to come in of an immense force of Zulus, subsequently estimated at 20,000, advancing rapidly on the camp. Colonel Pulleine reinforced his forward company of the 1/24th by another two companies, thus still further reducing the camp defences.

The Zulu attack developed quickly. Colonel Durnford, by this time five miles away with his Basutos, found himself in danger of being cut off from the camp and beat a hasty retreat. By 1 pm the Islandhlwana defence force was scattered over a wide front and the camp itself was virtually undefended.

Nothing could have played into the hands of the Zulus better than this dispersion of their enemies as they surged into the attack and swept over the camp. In the last hour of this sorry story many deeds of great valour were done and it is probable that several VCs might have been awarded had there been any survivors to tell the tale.

The British troops particularly sold their lives dearly but the casualties among the camp garrison were 1,329 killed, none wounded. The Zulus did not take prisoners. It was one of the worst disasters in British colonial history and it remained a source of bitter controversy for many years.

Two of the men who did escape were Private Sam Wassall and Private Westwood of the 80th (South Staffordshire Regiment). They both reached the Buffalo River pursued by Zulus. When Wassall saw Westwood struggling in the river and apparently drowning, he dismounted and went to his assistance. Then, under heavy Zulu fire, he dragged him out and again mounted his horse, taking Westwood with him. Samuel Wassall was awarded the Victoria Cross.

When the Zulus first got into the camp and it was clear that all was lost, the Adjutant of the 1/24th Regiment, Lieutenant Teignmouth Melvill, together with Lieutenant Nevill Coghill, also of the 1/24th, dashed out of the camp on horseback with the Queen's Colour of their regiment, hoping to be able to save it. As the road to Rorke's Drift was already in enemy hands these two subalterns struck across country to the Buffalo River. They were followed by Lieutenant Higginson of the Natal Native Contingent.

The Zulus, with their well-known agility in crossing rough country, pursued them closely. Lieutenant Coghill had sustained a severe injury to his knee which was a great handicap to him, but they both managed to reach the Buffalo River. Melvill plunged into the swiftly flowing water, horse and all, but was much encumbered by the Colour which was awkward to carry. He became separated from his horse but clung to the Colour with the help of Lieutenant Higginson.

Meanwhile, Coghill had arrived safely across the river with his horse, but seeing Melvill in difficulties he rode back to help him. By now the Zulus had reached the river bank in considerable force and opened heavy rifle fire on the three officers as they struggled in the river. Lieutenant Coghill's horse was killed and the Colour was swept away. Melvill and Coghill managed to reach the far bank in a state of great exhaustion. They were found next day with a ring of dead Zulus round them showing that they had sold their lives dearly.

King Edward VII awarded both of these officers the Victoria Cross. That of Lieutenant Melvill was given to his widow. Her elder son, Teignmouth Phillip Melvill, became an international polo player and commanded the 17th Lancers; the younger boy, Charles William, became a brigadier-general and commanded the 1st New Zealand Infantry Brigade.

There was considerable controversy as to what became of the Queen's Colour of the South Wales Borderers, most accounts saying that it was lost in the Buffalo River. But this is not so. A search party afterwards recovered the Colour from the river. Whilst the 1st Battalion South Wales Borderers was at Gosport in 1880, Queen Victoria expressed a wish to see the Colour. Accordingly, on 28 July of that year, Lieutenant-Colonel J. M. G. Tongue, with Lieutenants Weallens and Phipps, and an escort of Colour-Sergeants, carried the Colour to

Osborne, where Her Majesty attached a wreath of immortelles to the pole.

At Brecon Cathedral, in the Memorial Chapel of the South Wales Borderers, there rest:

i   the Chillianwallah Colours presented to the 1st Battalion 24th Regiment in 1825 (the Queen's Colour being a replacement of the original);

ii   their successors, the Isandhlwana Colours of the 1st Battalion 24th Regiment, presented in 1866;

iii   one Colour pole of the set of Colours presented to the 2nd Battalion 24th Regiment in May 1859 upon its being raised at Sheffield.

All the officers who carried these Colours in action were killed while defending them; an event which is perhaps unique in the annals of the British Army. In those days, of course, the regimental colours were carried in action and often acted as a rallying point and morale centre of the battalion. It was always a great honour to be a Colour bearer in or out of action.

The Zulus, flushed with victory after Isandlhwana, pressed on to the invasion of Natal but were stopped at Rorke's Drift on the River Tugela by a handful of men of the 2nd/24th (South Wales Borderers). In this little epic of British endurance, leadership and gallantry, eleven VCs were won, seven of them by the 2nd/24th.

When Colonel Glyn's Column had advanced into Zululand a commissariat post had been established at Rorke's Drift, which was due west of Isandhlwana. It consisted of two buildings built of stone and roofed with thatch. One of these was used as a store for ammunition and the other as a hospital. The garrison consisted of eight officers and 131 men, some eighty of them from the 24th, The South Wales Borderers. Of these 131, thirty-five were sick in hospital. The detachment of the 24th was commanded by Lieutenant Gonville Bromhead, aged thirty-five. He had joined the 24th as an Ensign and had served in the South African War of 1877-79. The post was commanded by Lieutenant John Rouse Marriott Chard of the Royal Engineers, aged thirty-two. There was a Surgeon-Major J. H. Reynolds in the post.

During the afternoon of 22 January, the guard posted at the river ferry saw two white men on the further bank signalling urgently to be taken across. They were Lieutenant Adendorf of the Natal Contingent and one of the Natal Carabiniers, survivors of the disaster at Isandhlwana. They gave warning that the Zulus were close behind them and making for Rorke's Drift.

Chard and Bromhead at once set every fit man to work on strengthening the defences. The buildings were loopholed; breast-works were constructed of mealie bags and biscuit tins. A number of fugitives from the Native Contingent had arrived and they helped with the work.

It was the Undi Corps, 3,500 strong, and comprising some of Cetywayo's finest warriors who, having slaughtered all the fugitives they could find from Isandhlwana, broke away to capture Rorke's Drift. Their advance guard was sighted at 4.20 pm and at once a number of the Native Contingent in the post, acutely aware of what had happened at Isandhlwana, slipped away and made for Natal. The garrison felt happier without them. This left a total of 104 officers, NCOs and men to defend the post, with thirty-five patients in the hospital.

Almost as soon as they arrived the Zulus attacked the post fiercely, attempting by sheer weight of numbers and complete disregard of death, to overrun the small garrison of the post. They were met by a steady and devastating fire which threw them back. When darkness fell the difficulties of the defence were much increased. The Zulus set fire to the thatched roof of the hospital but the defenders managed to remove most of the patients before they were forced to evacuate the building. This setback and the loss of some of their sick comrades only stiffened their resistance.

Privates John Williams and Henry Hook of the 2/24th were posted with Privates Joseph Williams and William Horrigan of the 1/24th in a distant room of the hospital, which they held until the Zulus burst open the door. They dragged out Joseph Williams with two patients and assegaied them. John Williams and Henry Hook, together with two patients, were the only men left alive in the ward. Keeping the enemy at bay they broke through three partitions of the hospital and brought out eight patients who would otherwise have been slaughtered by the Zulus. Privates Robert Jones and William Jones defended their ward in the hospital until six of their seven patients had been evacuated to safety. The seventh was assegaied by the Zulus.

All through the night the Zulus made every effort to overrun the little post. At last, at about 4 am, they drew off, leaving great piles of their dead and wounded strewn around the post. For twelve long hours the garrison, very heavily outnumbered, had resisted with the utmost courage and determination. The casualties were fifteen killed and twelve wounded, whilst the Zulus had lost 350 killed.

Gallantry of this nature is not possible without inspired leadership and this was given in full by John Chard and Gonville Bromhead, to both of whom the vc was awarded. The other vcs awarded to the South Wales Borderers, in addition to those already mentioned, were to Corporal William Allen and Private Frederick Hitch, both of whom were severely wounded. For his constant attendance to the wounded under fire Surgeon-Major Reynolds was awarded the vc, as was Assistant Commissary James Dalton and Corporal F. C. Schiess of the Natal Native Contingent. The latter had been wounded before the Zulu assault but yet took part in several counter-attacks with the bayonet. After his death it was discovered that he was of Swiss nationality.

Rorke's Drift will be remembered with pride as long as the history of British arms exists.

5

Three Father and Son VCS.

1. Lieutenant F. S. Roberts, Bengal Artillery, Indian Mutiny, January 1858, and Lieutenant the Hon. F. H. S. Roberts, King's Royal Rifle Corps, South African War, 15 December 1899.

Lord Roberts was one of the most famous soldiers of his time or of our history. He was a great hero of my youth but I met him only once, just three days before his death in France on Saturday, 14 November 1914, at the age of eighty-two. He had come out to visit the Indian troops and on Thursday the twelfth, as a subaltern in the 15th Sikhs, I had taken a small party for his inspection. It was on this day that he caught his fatal chill.

Frederick Sleigh Roberts was educated at Eton, Sandhurst and Addiscombe and was gazetted to the Bengal Artillery on 12 December 1851. On the occurrence of a vacancy in the Horse Artillery he was selected for it and became a lieutenant on 31 May 1857, just after the Indian Mutiny had started. He joined the Delhi Field Force and was appointed to the headquarters staff as Deputy Assistant Quartermaster General which in those days was very much an appointment with the fighting troops. His gallantry on many occasions had been most distinguished. Towards the end of 1857 he became attached to General Sir James Hope Grant's Cavalry Division.

While they were following up a body of mutineers on 2 January 1858 at Khodagunge, between Cawnpore and Delhi, Lieutenant Roberts joined in a cavalry charge, attaching himself to a squadron commanded by Major Younghusband. The mutineers turned and opened fire on the squadron at close range. Younghusband fell seriously wounded. Roberts cut down a rebel sepoy who was attacking a sowar with the

21

bayonet, and thereby saved the latter's life. He then pursued two sepoys who were making off with a standard. He cut down one of them with his sword; the other fired at him at point black range but his musket missed fire and Roberts rode off with the standard. For these two acts of gallantry he was awarded the vc.

This gallant young officer was to become one of the greatest and most beloved commanders in British history. Despite the fact that in the Mutiny he had become so affected by the sight of the aftermath of the butchery of British women and children in Cawnpore that he was filled with a fierce hatred of the mutineers, he afterwards played a large part in building up the magnificent new Indian Army which played such significant role, first in Indian frontier defence, and later in the critical early battles in France, and in Mesopotamia and the Middle East in the First World War.

Lieutenant the Hon. F. H. S. Roberts, Lord Roberts' only son, was born at Umballa, India, in 1872 and was commissioned in the King's Royal Rifle Corps on 10 June 1891. During the next four years he saw service on the north-west frontier of India and was mentioned in despatches. When his father was appointed to the Irish Command in 1895, having been given the baton of a Field-Marshal, his son Freddie came home to act as his ADC and the Roberts family had a very happy four years together.

On 11 October 1899 President Kruger declared war on Great Britain and the Boers scored some damaging early successes against the numerically weak British forces which did not at first exceed 22,000 men. Freddie went out to South Africa as ADC to General Penn, commanding Natal. General Sir Redvers Buller, vc, who had arrived in Cape Town on 31 October to take charge of the operations, suffered considerable criticism for his handling of the situation, though he was faced with enormous difficulties with very few troops.

On 8 December Lord Roberts, then over sixty-seven, placed his services at the disposal of the Government should it wish to appoint him in supreme command in South Africa. The Prime Minister, however, said he would keep the matter in mind but thought that Lord Roberts, though still very spry and fit, was too old for a field command. There followed a black week for Britain in South Africa. On 11 December General Gatacre was repulsed at Stormberg, on the fourteenth there was a reverse at Magersfontein and on the fifteenth Buller himself was beaten back with heavy losses in his attempt to cross the Tugela River at Colenso.

When news of this disaster reached Lord Roberts he drafted a telegram to the Secretary of State for War expressing his opinion that unless some radical change in command took place the British would be forced to make an ignominious peace with the Boers. Hardly had he sent the telegram when he received a telegram from General Buller to say that his son, Freddie, had been killed at Colenso and had been recommended for a posthumous VC. His death was a shattering blow to the Roberts family.

Hardly had these events taken place when Roberts received a telegram from the Secretary of State for War asking him to go to London immediately and be prepared to go to South Africa as Supreme Commander without delay.

The battle of Colenso, fought on 15 December 1899, was one of the darkest hours of the South African War. It was yet another attempt to relieve Ladysmith, but although the force which General Buller led into action was the largest which any British general had commanded since the Battle of the Alma in the Crimea, he found the skilfully prepared Boer defences too strong for him. British troops fought valiantly and sustained heavy casualties. Seven VCs were won in this grim action on 15 December 1899.

The really dramatic story of Colenso centres round the loss of the two field batteries, the 14th and the 66th, and all seven of the VCs, including that of Freddie Roberts, were directly concerned with this incident. In their eagerness to advance and engage the enemy these two batteries had unlimbered and came into action against Fort Wylie, which was the centre of the main Boer position, oblivious of the fact that the forward Boer trenches at the foot of the hill were only 500 to 700 yards distant from the gun positions. At once a hail of bullets swept over the two batteries and men and horses fell in heaps. The gunners continued to serve the guns as unconcernedly as if they were firing a salute at a ceremonial parade. Then the Boer automatic quick-firing guns found the range and the carnage became appalling.

Colonel Long, in command of the artillery, fell with one bullet through his arm and another through his liver, but he protested loudly when they dragged him back under the shelter of a little donga. Soon the situation was such that so many men had been hit that the guns could neither be served nor moved, as the horses were shot down at once when they attempted to bring up a limber. One gun was still being served by four men who refused to quit until they were all killed. One of the gunners was found afterwards with sixty-four wounds in his body.

General Buller and General Clery, hearing of the desperate position of the two batteries, had come forward to the ravine where the limbers were situated and General Buller called for volunteers to serve the guns. Among those who responded to the call were the General's three ADCs: Captain Walter Congreve of the Rifle Brigade, Captain Henry Schofield, Royal Field Artillery, and Lieutenant the Hon. Frederick Roberts, King's Royal Rifle Corps. Corporal George Nurse, Royal Field Artillery, and six gunners went with them.

This little party tried to take two limbers up to the guns, galloping them forward at full speed through a hail of bullets and shells. They succeeded in bringing back two of the guns, but at fearful cost. Roberts fell mortally wounded. Congreve was wounded and his horse was hit by three bullets. He and Corporal Nurse turned back to try to bring in Roberts. Schofield played a major part in bringing back the only two guns which were saved, as did Private George Ravenhill of the Royal Scots Fusiliers.

Congreve, Schofield, Roberts, Nurse and Ravenhill were all awarded the VC, as also was Captain Hamilton Lyster Reed of the 7th Battery Royal Field Artillery, who brought along three gun teams from his own battery and made a gallant but unsuccessful attempt to save some more of the guns. He was wounded, as were five of the thirteen men who rode with him. Out of the twenty-one horses they took out, thirteen, including Reed's own charger, were killed before they were half way.

One of the most gallant VCs won on this day was that awarded to Major William Babtie, CMG, of the Royal Army Medical Corps. When a message was sent back for medical assistance for the wounded who were lying out in the donga, he rode out there under heavy fire, his pony being hit three times. When he arrived he found them lying in a sheltered corner of the donga. He attended to them all, going out into the open from one to another under a hail of fire. Later in the day he went out with Captain Congreve to bring in Lieutenant Roberts who was lying mortally wounded on the veldt.

Babtie was a fine-looking man, who had been educated at Glasgow University. After distinguished service in the First World War he finished up as a Lieutenant-General and Honorary Surgeon to the King.

The gun which Freddie Roberts had died to save was afterwards presented to his father, Lord Roberts, by the War Office and on it, fourteen years later, the great Field-Marshal's coffin was carried at his funeral.

2. *Captain W. N. Congreve, The Rifle Brigade, South African War, 15 December 1899, and Brevet-Major W. La Touche Congreve, DSO, MC, The Rifle Brigade, France, 6 to 20 July 1916.*

It is curious that the second example of father and son VCs follows immediately on the first and once again it was the father who survived and the son who was killed.

William La Touche Congreve had already greatly distinguished himself in the operations in France and Belgium and had been awarded the DSO, the MC and the Legion of Honour. He had been recommended for the VC when he won his DSO in March 1916 at St Eloi for the most conspicuous bravery in consolidating a newly won position and capturing seventy-two Germans under the most difficult and dangerous conditions. No other officer had previously ever won the VC, DSO and MC.

During the fourteen days of July preceeding his death in action on the Somme he had constantly inspired those around him by numerous acts of gallantry in critical periods of the operations. As Brigade Major he not only conducted battalions up to their positions, but, despite the fact that he was suffering severely from the effects of gas and from being heavily shelled, he showed supreme courage in assisting the medical officer at his brigade headquarters to remove the wounded to places of safety. He was finally shot and killed instantly. He was buried at Corbie on the Somme, his father, who was then a corps commander in France, attending his funeral.

3. *Major C. J. S. Gough, 5th Bengal European Cavalry, Indian Mutiny, 15 and 18 August 1857, 27 January 1858 and 23 February 1858, and Captain and Brevet-Major J. S. Gough, The Rifle Brigade, Somaliland, 22 April 1903.*

The Goughs were a very famous v c family for, in addition to this father and son, Major C. J. S. Gough's brother, Lieutenant H. H. Gough of the 1st Bengal European Cavalry (19th Horse), also won the v c in the Indian Mutiny. The brothers were considered to be two of the most brilliant young cavalry leaders of their day. Charles, the elder of the two, had already distinguished himself at the siege of Delhi and been mentioned in despatches. He was then transferred to Hodson's Irregular Horse and accompanied them with Sir Colin Campbell's force in the second relief of Lucknow, for which service he was mentioned three times in despatches. He then took part with his regiment in the operations in the Cawnpore district where he was wounded, but he recovered sufficiently to take part in the final capture of Lucknow. For his services in the campaign he received a brevet majority and the Victoria Cross.

The Cross was awarded to him for four acts of bravery. First, on 15 August 1857, in which he saved his brother, who was wounded, and killed two of the enemy; second, on 18 August, when he led a troop of the Guides Cavalry in a charge and cut down two of the enemy's sowars; third, on 27 January 1858, when he personally killed three of the enemy in a charge; fourth, on 23 February, when he rescued a brother officer and killed his assailant.

Hugh Gough, the younger brother, served throughout the Mutiny, and was present at the siege and capture of Delhi. He took part in the engagement at Bolundshadur and Futtehpur as well as in the relief of Lucknow, where he was severely wounded and had two horses shot under him. On 25 February 1858 he showed a brilliant example to his regiment when ordered to charge the enemy's guns. He was always in the forefront of a battle. He received a brevet majority as well as the Victoria Cross.

Captain John Gough, the son of Charles Gough, v c, and the nephew of General Sir Hugh Gough, v c, won his Cross in Somaliland on 22 April 1903, when two other v cs were won. John Gough was in command of a column and rescued two mortally wounded officers when

the column was attacked by a large force of Somalis. The Goughs
seemed to bear charmed lives.

6

Le Cateau, France.

On 22 August 1914 the British Expeditionary Force, for ever after known as 'the Old Contemptibles', had occupied the line of the canal west of Mons on the extreme west of the French armies. This move by the BEF came as a complete surprise to the advancing Germans who ran into General Smith-Dorrien's 2nd Corps and were brought to a full stop by the murderous rifle fire of the British infantry. The French on the right however, had sustained a severe setback and were forced to retreat and the British had to conform. In this way the historic retreat from Mons began.

The Germans were following hard on their heels. Behind the British lay the big Forest of Mormal and the two British Corps, the 1st, under Sir Douglas Haig, and the 2nd, under Sir Horace Smith-Dorrien, passed on either side of it. The long forced marches from the detrainment stations to the forward concentration areas, followed almost immediately by long and disheartening retreats for which the troops could see no reason, the extreme heat and the hard cobbled roads were a great ordeal for the infantry. It must be remembered that nearly fifty per cent of them were reservists just called up and not in hard condition, and that applied to the horses, too.

The greatest German pressure was directed against 2nd Corps, and by the evening of the twenty-fifth a serious situation had arisen. The troops arrived at their bivouacs late in the evening, in no condition to continue the retreat without food and rest and with the German advanced guards pressing close upon them. It was quite clear to Smith-Dorrien that unless they continued their withdrawal during the night of 25/26 August a dangerous situation, jeopardizing the whole safety of the BEF could not be avoided. All subordinate commanders considered that a further withdrawal that night was out of the question. During the early hours of the twenty-sixth, therefore, Smith-Dorrien decided that he must stand and fight, give the enemy 'a bloody nose' and then continue his retreat. At 3 am he issued orders accordingly.

There followed the epic battle of Le Cateau in which the British, hopelessly outnumbered, gave the mighty German Army a knock which they remembered for a very long time and which saved the BEF from the certainty of a great disaster.

Five VCs resulted from this critical engagement on 26 August. Two were won by Major Charles Yate and Lance-Corporal Frederick William Holmes of the 2nd Battalion Yorkshire Light Infantry, and the other three by Captain Douglas Reynolds and Drivers John Henry Drain and Frederick Luke of the 37th Battery Royal Field Artillery.

Major Yate had been a Sandhurst cadet and was forty-two when he won his Cross. The company he commanded maintained its position to the very end and when all the other officers were killed or wounded, Yate led his nineteen survivors in a last desperate charge against the enemy, in which he was severely wounded. He was picked up by the Germans and died as a prisoner of war. Lance Corporal Holmes supported his captain throughout and assisted in driving a gun out of action by taking the place of a driver who had been wounded.

Captain Reynolds and Drivers Drain and Luke were with the 37th Battery, attached to 15th Brigade Royal Field Artillery, which performed prodigies of valour with all the guns pushed well forward to give the fullest support to the infantry. They caused havoc in the ranks of the German infantry but the situation of the whole brigade became increasingly hazardous as the day wore on and the British gunners' losses in men and horses were terrible. It was estimated that over a hundred guns, besides many machine-guns, were massed against the Suffolks and 15th Brigade Royal Field Artillery.

Seeing that two abandoned howitzers of 37th Battery must fall into enemy hands, Captain Douglas Reynolds, the Battery Commander, obtained permission from the CRA, who was on the spot, to call for volunteers to rescue them. Accompanied by Lieutenants E. G. Earle and W. D. Morgan, both of 37th Battery, Captain Reynolds led two teams to bring out the guns. Despite the fact that the German infantry was only a hundred yards away, they managed to limber up the two guns. One entire team was immediately shot down and Driver Godley, the driver of the central pair of the other team, was killed. Reynolds, however, kept the remainder in hand and, with the assistance of Drivers Luke and Drain, brought one of the guns safely away.

At 2.45 pm a mass of German infantry swept over the doomed right flank of the 2nd Corps defence and the 2nd Suffolk Regiment was overwhelmed, together with the men of the Manchesters, the Argylls and 15th Brigade RFA, who were with them. The 52nd Battery RFA fought to the last round and the last man.

By 5 pm 2nd Corps was able to resume its retreat with the rear-guards all in position. By 6 pm a drizzling rain had set in and the light had begun to fail. The enemy's pursuit died away. There was, of course, considerable confusion and congestion on the roads, with infantry, guns, transport and ambulances all converging on to them. But the men marched on steadily. They were tired and hungry but, rightly, very proud of themselves. General Smith-Dorrien who, towards evening, watched the 5th Division pass along the road, likened them to a crowd coming away from a race meeting – men smoking their pipes, apparently quite unconcerned. Out of the 50,000 men engaged at Le Cateau the total loss did not exceed 8000, which shows that 2nd Corps was far from being overwhelmed.

On 26 August 1914 the most powerful and best-equipped military machine the world had ever seen had been held in a bitter encounter by a British force much less than half its strength. At the end of the day the attackers had been so mauled that the pursuing German Army entirely changed its character. It ceased to be a reckless, thrusting, triumphant force and became much more respectful and hesitant. In fact, Smith-Dorrien took a big decision at Le Cateau entirely on his own and did just what he said he would do: he gave the Germans 'a bloody nose' and then broke off the engagement and continued his withdrawal.

7

France, 1914–15.

When the First World War started the 9th Lancers, together with the 4th Dragoon Guards and the 18th Hussars, made up into the 2nd Cavalry Brigade, sailed for France on 15 August. The 9th comprised thirty officers and 588 other ranks, with 613 horses. It is remarkable and probably unique that the regiment had four pairs of brothers, including the Grenfells (Captain F. O. and Lieutenant R. N. Grenfell).

The Grenfell twins, Francis and Riversdale – who was generally known to his friends as 'Rivy' – were two fine young men who could hardly have been more popular and admired. They were born on 4 September 1880 and were educated at Eton. Francis was in the Eton cricket eleven in 1899 and in the Eton and Harrow match of that year helped to create a record when he and H. K. Longman made 170 runs for the first wicket.

On leaving Eton, Francis had joined the 3rd Battalion Seaforth Highlanders and was then gazetted to the 60th Rifles and saw service with them in the South African War. After this he went to India with the 60th and having arrived there he exchanged into the 9th Lancers. Francis was not merely a dashing cavalry leader; he was a very keen student of his profession of arms and a first-class trainer of his men.

In the years leading up to the First World War the brothers played polo in almost every country where polo was played. By 1911 they had both attained an eight handicap which put them among the top players in the world. Rivy had also taken up pigsticking in India and, in 1905, had won the much-coveted Kadir Cup.

By 6 pm on the 18 August the 9th Lancers were in billets at Jeumont, five miles north-east of Mauberge. On the twenty-first the regiment moved to Hermignies, four miles south-east of Mons and had its first sight of the war when a patrol caught a glimpse of Uhlans. Late on the next night the regiment received orders to move across the rear of the British Army from the right flank to the left, to support the left of 2nd Corps, which was holding the line of the Mons-Condé Canal.

The horses slid and stumbled along the paved roads in the pitch darkness but although there were several falls no man or horse was seriously hurt. All along the route sleepy villagers turned out in their night attire to see them pass. At last, just before dawn on the twenty-third, the regiment halted in a wet field south of Thulin. Men and horses snatched a quick meal before bedding down. But not for long. At 8 am reveille sounded and soon after midday the sound of gun and rifle fire from the north announced that British infantry were engaged with the Germans along the line of the Mons Canal. It was the first battle of the war and the 9th found itself in anything but ideal cavalry country – densely populated, with coal mines, smoky villages, towering slag heaps, railway embankments and endless wire fences. If they wondered what this war was going to be like, they soon found it was no place for mounted troops.

At first light Captain Francis Grenfell's B Squadron moved forward to reconnoitre and ran into some Germans holding a bridge over the canal. They sustained their first casualties of the war. At 9 am, in accordance with orders, they retired at a leisurely pace, finding ample cover in the close country with its many sunken roads. The 9th then experienced their first shelling from German batteries which found their range with remarkable speed and accuracy, causing several casualties, Francis Grenfell having his horse shot under him. They continued to withdraw without serious interference and by midday had rejoined the 2nd Cavalry Brigade, where the regiment halted, sending out patrols.

The situation became ominous as a whole German Army Corps was advancing rapidly and threatening to envelop 5th Division on the left of 2nd Corps. The GOC 5th Division sent an urgent appeal for help to General Allenby, commanding the cavalry. The 2nd Cavalry Brigade was ordered to go back and attempt to restore the situation. But before this move could take effect long lines of advancing German infantry suddenly appeared.

The 4th Dragoon Guards, with A and B Squadrons of the 9th, were ordered to charge. In front of them lay a gentle rising slope, cut up by sunken lanes, railway cuttings and quickset hedges, and covered with corn stooks, behind which the enemy took cover as the cheering cavalry galloped towards them. They swept over the sunken road, spearing one or two Germans, before being struck by shell fire and a hail of bullets. Losing men at every stride, and with no visible objective, they suddenly came up against a long wire fence. Men and horses fell in all directions under the withering fire of the German infantry. This charge was as gallant, but just as futile, as other attempts in history when cavalry have charged unbroken infantry, in country utterly unfavourable for mounted action. But its sheer audacity and unexpectedness had checked the German advance and given a much-needed respite to 5th Division.

A sugar factory and some slag heaps about 1400 yards south-east of Quievrain afforded a rallying point for the shattered A and B Squadrons of the 9th and, together with some men of the 4th Dragoon Guards, they dismounted and took up a position under command of Captains Grenfell and Lucas-Tooth.

It was not until 2.30 pm that the Germans resumed their advance under cover of heavy artillery fire. The little band of the 9th Lancers then withdrew towards Elouges. Captain Grenfell had been wounded twice, in the hand and the thigh. Hard by the railway embankment, south-east of the village, the 119th Field Battery, their personnel and their horses much depleted by the German shell fire, were trying vainly to manhandle their guns back to some shelter. The Battery Commander, Lieutenant-Colonel Ernest Wright Alexander, appealed to Francis Grenfell to help him save the guns. Grenfell at once responded and called upon eleven officers of the 9th to help him. The volunteers for this desperate venture, together with the battery commander and some dozen gunners, ran across two fields and manhandled the guns back under cover. They had to be turned and lifted over the dead bodies of the gun teams under heavy fire. Fresh horses and drivers were then able to gallop the guns away to safety.

Despite having been wounded once more, Captain Grenfell rode nearly ten miles back with his squadron before collapsing from exhaustion. Grenfell and Alexander were both awarded the Victoria Cross. Alexander was born at Liverpool in 1870 and was educated at Harrow.

He was commissioned in the Royal Artillery in 1889. He survived the war and retired as a brigadier-general.

During the next three weeks, before stabilized trench warfare began, the 9th Lancers were engaged in several mounted reconnaissance actions, in one of which, on 14 September, Rivy Grenfell was killed. Francis Grenfell rejoined the regiment, with his wounds healed, on 12 October but on 30 October he was wounded again when the 9th were engaged in a dismounted role near Messines. Before this action their strength had been brought up to twenty-seven officers and 416 non-commissioned officers and men, which was not much below their full establishment of 531. But in this battle they were heavily attacked by two German infantry regiments and lost three-quarters of their officers and over a third of their other ranks.

Francis Grenfell was invalided home and had his V C presented to him by the King on 21 February 1915. He was so eager to return to his regiment that he left England on 17 April, as soon as he was allowed to do so, and he went through all the grim fighting around Ypres in April and May.

On 22 April 1915 the Germans had first used gas – the heavier than air chlorine, discharged from cylinders – in the Ypres Salient with deadly and devastating effect against totally unprotected troops. Two days later, as a subaltern in the 15th Sikhs, I had taken part in the Lahore Division counter-attack to restore the situation. I knew, therefore, from first hand the deadly effect of this choking death. Towards the beginning of May gas masks had been issued to the troops in the salient, but I was only too glad that the wind remained in our favour and I never had to trust my life to one.

The regimental history of the 9th Lancers records: 'Here, in the Salient on 24 May, the Regiment underwent its greatest day of glory, and of sorrow, of the whole war.' They had been experiencing some grim trench warfare assignments in this difficult and dangerous part of the front and had suffered a steady drain of casualties, particularly of officers. They had been almost made up to full establishment when their next tour of duty in the front line began on the night of Sunday, 23 May. It must be remembered that a cavalry regiment, on a much lower establishment than an infantry battalion, and with all its horses to look after, could not take over an infantry battalion's trench sector. In this case, the

9th, who could put only 350 rifles into the line, were reinforced by detachments from other units – 520 men of the 4th Green Howards and 5th Durham Light Infantry.

Thus reinforced the 9th Lancers took over 500 yards of the 9th Infantry Brigade sector astride the Menin Road, south-east of Hooge. With such an odd collection of units this relief in the dark was no easy matter, but the 9th Lancers co-ordinated matters splendidly. Captain Grenfell, commanding B Squadron with 300 men, took over the left portion astride the road. Captain A. N. Edwards with 150 men in A Squadron held the right portion, which included a blind-alley sap running forward almost into the enemy trench. Captain R. L. Benson with C Squadron was in support 200 yards behind the centre.

At 3 am next day, almost before the relief had been completed, the Germans sent up four red flares which was the signal for a furious artillery bombardment, with which they released clouds of gas on the whole of the 5th Corps front. There was little wind and the gas hung about in full density for over an hour and remained after that in hollows and among the trees. The makeshift British respirators became so saturated with gas that they afforded no protection. When, immediately following the gas, four divisions of German infantry left their trenches and advanced they were met with fierce resistance. Only on the extreme northern flank, in the Wieltje area and at the southern end, did they make a break in the British defence. The effects of this latter success would have been serious but for the splendid defence put up by the 9th Lancers and the infantry attached to them. This action checked the further progress of the enemy.

Drenched with gas and pulverized by trench mortar bombs, A Squadron's position on the right sector became untenable and had to be abandoned. C Squadron was hurried forward to occupy it. Part of the left sector, held by B Squadron, also had to be abandoned but was reoccupied later when the gas had cleared by two companies of the 2nd Buffs and a squadron of the 15th Hussars from the reserve. Casualties had been heavy; men were reeling about, clutching their throats, blind and falling unconscious from the effects of the gas. Captain Grenfell's Squadron had only a handful of men left fit to fight. Francis Grenfell himself was mortally wounded and died a few minutes later. The Germans, having broken through on the north, were pouring in a flood past the left flank, down the Menin road towards Ypres.

This dangerous incursion was eventually checked but was succeeded by a critical situation on the right. Largely owing to the stout resistance offered by the 9th and their attached troops, the German attack lost its momentum and was finally halted. The 4th Hussars and the 5th Lancers were gradually taking over from what was left of the 9th Lancers and in the early morning of the twenty-eighth the survivors stumbled along the Menin road and through the ruin that was Ypres. Their clothes were caked with mud and their faces yellow from the gas, but the highest tributes were paid to their bravery by the corps commander. Eight of the thirteen officers had become casualties. Of the rank and file thirty-three men were killed or died of wounds, seventy-two were wounded and 103 gassed – 208 casualties out of the 350 who had gone into the line.

The 9th Lancers' survivors of this epic little battle took back with them the body of their much beloved vc, Francis Grenfell, and buried him in Viamertinghe churchyard. He left his vc to his regiment, the 9th Lancers.

In the meantime, on 25 April, Captain Francis Alexander Caron Scrimger of the Canadian Army Medical Service (attached 14th Battalion Royal Montreal Regiment) had won his vc in the Ypres Salient. Throughout the fierce fighting which followed the Germans' first use of gas on 22 April, the 13th and 14th Battalions were fiercely engaged and suffered heavy casualties. Both these Canadian battalions had their mettle tested to a supreme degree.

The 14th Battalion's dressing station was right up close to the line and the wounded were pouring in from several different battalions. For three days and three nights Captain Scrimger and his stretcher-bearer section worked unceasingly among the Canadian and French casualties. There was no time to eat or sleep; the badly wounded had to be dressed and the men made as comfortable as possible. In one afternoon and evening more than 400 wounded passed through his dressing station. On the third day it was considered advisable to move the station further back. When all but fifteen of the wounded had been removed to safety the Germans put down a massive bombardment with incendiary bombs, which soon had the dressing station in a mass of flames. It was then that Captain Scrimger and his staff accomplished the seemingly impossible task of removing the fifteen helpless men. Assisted by volunteers they rescued the men and carried them on their backs to safety. Francis Scrimger carried a severely wounded officer out of the dressing station and when he could go no further, he remained with the patient under fire until help could be obtained. This little episode was a supreme example of endurance and utter selflessness. Scrimger survived the war and died in Montreal on 15 February 1937.

8

The Battle of Neuve Chapelle and the Action at Hill 60.

Neuve Chapelle in March 1915 was the first of the battles to be fought on the Western Front after the armies had settled down into conditions of continuous lines of trench systems, protected by fields of barbed wire and flanked by deadly concealed machine-gun nests which, together, caused such a blood bath in so many offensive operations. The queen of the battlefield was undoubtedly the Vickers machine-gun.

Despite all the theories of post-war writers and critics there was only one way of conducting a major offensive operation on the Western Front and that was by breaking through the forward trench system and then exploiting success through the gap which had been created. The methods of making the breakthrough were strictly limited. Apart from the introduction of a new weapon, such as poison gas or the tank, the only way was by bringing to bear on the enemy wire and trenches such a massive weight of artillery fire that the wire was cut and the defenders' forward defences so shattered that the attacking waves of troops could capture them and then exploit the breakthrough. The premier offensive arm was the artillery, and the essential arm for the capture and consolidation of ground, and for defending the trench system, was the infantry. The success of such an operation depended to a very large extent on meticulous planning of every detail.

On 10 March, after a thirty-five minute bombardment which was generally most effective, four divisions (Lahore, Merrut, 8th and 7th) attacked on a two-mile front. On the first day the German defence was shattered and Neuve Chapelle captured, but the Germans recoverd with their usual speed and fanatical bravery. On this day two VCs were won. The first went to Rifleman Gobar Singh Negi of the 2nd Battalion 39th Garhwal Rifles. The Garhwalis were great fighters and this was a fine battalion. But they had taken a wrong direction in the early morning mist and attacked a portion of the German defences which had not been dealt with by the preliminary bombardment. Despite this, they forced their way most gallantly through the unbroken wire and captured 200 yards of German trenches, although at terrible cost. All the six British officers leading the assault were killed and several others (out of a total establishment of twelve) were wounded. With no British officers left the battalion held the ground it had won - a splendid achievement.

Gobar Singh Negi was one of the bayonet men with a bombing party. He was the first man to go round every traverse, killing several of the enemy and forcing a number of others to surrender. This brave soldier was afterwards killed and awarded his vc posthumously.

The other vc awarded on the first day went to Private William Buckingham of the 2nd Battalion The Leicestershire Regiment for conspicuous acts of bravery in rescuing wounded men under heavy fire.

Throughout 11 March the Indian Corps and the 4th Corps used their reserve formations to press forward against increasing German resistance. During the night of the 11/12 March the Germans brought forward reinforcements and on the twelfth they counter-attacked fiercely all along the line. It was on this day that the seven other vcs were won.

Corporal C. R. Noble and Company Sergeant-Major H. Daniels of the 2nd Battalion the Rifle Brigade courted certain death when they ran forward to cut a way for their company through the wire entanglement. Both of them were dangerously wounded but not before their gallant action had enabled the German trench to be taken. Corporal Noble died of his wounds and was awarded his Cross posthumously; Daniels recovered and was granted a commission on 21 July and awarded the Military Cross for a further act of bravery at Fromelles on 2 March 1916.

Two men of the 1st Battalion Grenadier Guards, Lance-Corporal Wilfrid Fuller and Private Edward Barber, performed two quite individual and remarkable acts of gallantry. Fuller, seeing a party of the enemy trying to escape, killed the leading man with a bomb, whereupon the remainder, numbering about fifty, surrendered to him, although he was entirely alone at the time. Barber's action was equally dramatic. He ran ahead of the grenade company to which he belonged and bombed the enemy with such effect that a large number of them surrendered to him. When the grenade company reached him they found him quite alone and unsupported, surrounded by his captives. Private Barber was killed a week later and was awarded his Cross posthumously.

Three other gallant VCs were also won on this day by Corporal W. Anderson, 2nd Battalion The Yorkshire Regiment (Green Howards), posthumous; Captain C. C. Foss, DSO, 2nd Battalion The Bedfordshire Regiment and Private J. Rivers, 1st Battalion Notts and Derby Regiment (Sherwood Foresters).

During 13 and 14 March both sides consolidated their new positions. Had the British been content with the gains they had made on the first day, Neuve Chapelle would have been a considerable victory. As it was the Germans regained much of their lost ground. General Rawlinson's policy of 'Bite and hold' as opposed to 'Bite and exploit' was undoubtedly sound, at any rate at this stage of the war.

The action at Hill 60, two miles east of Ypres, on 20/21 April 1915, was certainly one of the most heroic in the history of the British Army. Hill 60 was just a heap of earth but it was important because it afforded an artillery observation post from which a large portion of the front could be commanded.

On 17 April the British had exploded several mines under the hill, after which, under cover of heavy artillery fire, it was stormed with the bayonet. The enemy counter-attacked strongly and fierce hand-to-hand fighting ensued, as a result of which the Germans regained most of the hill. The British, however, again took the hill in a bayonet assault. The Germans returned to the attack and throughout the nineteenth and twentieth the hill was subjected to a terrific artillery battering, followed by infantry and bombing attacks.

This action won three VCs for the 1st Battalion East Surrey Regiment and one for the 9th Battalion London Regiment of the Territorial Force.

On 20 April Lieutenant George Roupell was commanding a company of the East Surreys in a front line trench of Hill 60, which was subjected to a very severe bombardment throughout the day. Towards evening strong German bombing parties worked their way forward along the communication trenches, linking their front line with the British position. Lieutenant Roupell, though wounded in several places, remained at his post and led his company in repelling a strong German assault. After having his wounds dressed he insisted on returning to his company. He then went back for reinforcements and with their assistance held the position through the night, until his battalion was relieved next morning. Roupell was one of the few survivors of his company.

Private Edward Dwyer won the second of the East Surrey VCs, when, at the age of nineteen, he displayed great gallantry in holding a trench single-handed and keeping the Germans at bay with bombs at a critical time in the Hill 60 engagement.

The third East Surrey VC was won by 2nd Lieutenant Handley Geary. On both 20 and 21 April he held the left crater of his company's position which was subjected to very heavy artillery fire, and afterwards to repeated bomb attacks. At one time Handley Geary used a rifle with great effect and at another threw hand-grenades with entire disregard for his own safety. It was largely owing to his gallantry and inspired leadership that this portion of his battalion's front was held.

The fourth Hill 60 VC was won by 2nd Lieutenant Harold Woolley, 9th Battalion The London Regiment (Queen Victoria's Rifles). This became the first unit of the Territorial Force to provide a VC. Two companies of the Queen Victoria's Rifles had come to the rescue at a very critical moment in the struggle for the Hill. Both the company commanders had been killed and two-thirds of the men had become casualties. It was doubtful whether the survivors could endure it any longer. Woolley put new heart into them and saved the situation. Although he became the only surviving officer, he successfully resisted all attacks on his position.

The Reverend Harold Woolley, as he afterwards became, also won the MC in 1919 and served again in 1943 during the Second World War. When the Victoria Cross Association was formed in 1956 Harold Woolley became the United Kingdom Vice-Chairman.

Four days after this epic fight at Hill 60 the first Canadian VC of the war was won by Captain Edward Bellew of the 7th Canadian Infantry Battalion of the British Columbia Regiment. The incident occurred near Keerselaere during the German attack on the Ypres Salient.

Captain Bellew, as battalion machine-gun officer, had two guns in action when the enemy's attack broke in full force against the 7th Canadians. Reinforcements were sent forward but they were surrounded and destroyed. The enemy established itself in strength less than a hundred yards away. No further assistance was in sight and the rear of the position was also threatened. Nevertheless, Captain Bellew and Sergeant Peerless, each operating a gun, decided to stay where they were and fight it out. Sergeant Peerless was killed and although Captain Bellew was wounded, he managed to stand up and maintained his fire until his ammunition ran out and the Germans rushed the position. Then he smashed his machine-gun, seized a rifle and, fighting to the end, was taken prisoner.

9

Gallipoli, 1915.

There are few more hazardous operations of war for any troops to undertake than a sea landing on some foreign shore, especially when the all-important element of surprise is lacking and the landing place is covered by fire from well-chosen trenches and heavily protected by sea and land mines and underwater wire. When, in addition, the defenders are brave and resolute men, as the Turks turned out to be, ready to die in defence of their homeland, then indeed none but the finest troops can hope to effect a lodgement. All these factors applied to the landings at w and v beaches at Gallipoli.

In addition to the six vcs awarded to the Lancashire Fusiliers on 25 April, nine more vcs were awarded for the V Beach landing, six of which went to the Royal Navy and three to the Army. Such was the gallantry shown by the troops in these desperate actions that many more vcs were probably deserved.

Gallipoli was a very rushed operation. It had been intended originally that the Royal Navy should force its way alone through the Dardanelles, but these narrow waters lent themselves to the laying of mines and it soon became apparent that a substantial military force would also be needed. By that time the all-important element of surprise had been completely lost and the defenders knew within fairly narrow limits where the attacks were likely to come, there being really only four main beaches. The Turks made use of all the time available to make these beaches as impregnable as possible with underwater wire, covered by well-sited and carefully concealed machine-guns. The British naval guns to support the landings were formidable and awe-inspiring but their flat trajectory made them unsuitable for searching out the Turkish machine-gun nests; in order to avoid hitting their own troops, they had to lengthen their range just when the attackers most needed their support.

At the outbreak of war in 1914 the 1st Battalion Lancashire Fusiliers was stationed at Karachi, India. In October 1914 they had started for home. Their red uniforms created quite a sensation among a population which had only seen soldiers in khaki since the beginning of the war. Now, re-equipped and completely up to full strength, they had arrived in Mudros as part of the 86th Brigade of the 29th Division. The other battalions of the brigade were the 2nd Royal Fusiliers, the 1st Royal Munster Fusiliers and the 1st Royal Dublin Fusiliers. They were indeed a *corps d'elite*, all formed from regiments in overseas garrisons which had been kept at full strength.

W Beach, the objective allotted to the Lancashire Fusiliers, was described by General Sir Ian Hamilton in his despatches as follows:

W Beach consists of a strip of deep, powdery sand, some 350 yards long and from fifteen to forty yards wide. On either flank of the beach the ground rises precipitately; but in the centre, a number of sand dunes afford a more gradual aspect to the ridge overlooking the sea. Much time and ingenuity had been employed by the Turks in turning this landing place into a death-trap. Close to the water's edge a broad wire entanglement extended the whole length of the shore and a supplementary barbed wire network lay concealed under the surface of the sea in the shallows. The high ground overlooking the beach was strongly fortified with trenches to which the gully afforded a natural covered approach. A number of machine-guns were also cunningly tucked away into holes in the cliff so as to be immune from naval bombardment whilst they were converging their fire upon the wire entanglements.

The Turks considered the defence to be quite impregnable. The wonder was not that the gallant Fusiliers failed to reach all their objectives, but that any of them got ashore at all.

If Sir Ian Hamilton had known all this beforehand would he have still ordered the landing there ? It was a difficult problem. The recognized beaches were by far the easiest to land on from ships' boats and best for the build-up of the following troops. Moreover, they were the easiest targets for the ships' guns. But they were certain to be the most strongly defended. I have always been of the opinion that many more landings should have been made by smaller forces in more difficult localities and then efforts made to capture the more obvious and heavily defended beaches from behind. The presence of the underwater wire had been clearly shown in the aerial photos and was a constant nightmare to Sir Ian Hamilton which became a dreadful reality on 25 April as the unfortunate troops became enmeshed in it. The Navy at home had certain contraptions which could have dealt with it but these Gallipoli landings had to be launched, under pressure from the British Cabinet, with such undue haste. Two or three submarines might have blown up the underwater wire with their torpedoes.

Whatever forebodings the higher command and staff had about the landings, the Fleet and the Army were in the highest spirits as D Day approached. Mudros harbour, where some 200 ships were assembled, looked like a holiday regatta. Bands played in the ships, the men were cheering and even the weather conditions improved; by midnight on 24 April the sea had calmed and a bright moon shone over the surface of the Aegean. Three companies of the Lancashire Fusiliers had embarked in the cruiser HMS *Euryalus,* with D Company in HMS *Implacable.* The officers and men were warmly welcomed on board by the Royal Navy. Before dawn the men were roused and given a meal while the ships took up their action stations for the preliminary bombardment in which 300 guns took part.

At 4 am the Fusiliers transferred into ships' cutters, in tows of six for each company. It was a tight fit to get the men in as each soldier was burdened with equipment weighing seventy pounds, which included three days' rations and 200 rounds of ammunition. The young naval midshipmen in charge of the steamboats came alongside and took the tows in charge. At 5 am, when the boats were clear of the ships, the bombardment began. The shelling was so intense and concentrated that it seemed that no living thing could survive in the target area nor any obstacle remain. Just before 6 am the tows headed for the shore, the steamboats cast off and the ships' boats were rowed in by the four naval ratings to each boat. As they came closer to the shore they could see that a belt of wire stretching across the beach had not been touched by the bombardment. What they could not see was that the Turks' machine-gun nests and rifle pits on the reverse side of the slopes overlooking the beach had also not been touched by the flat trajectory naval guns. Nor could they see the underwater wire until the boats reached it.

The Turks held their fire until the boats had fouled the underwater wire. Then a murderous fire was opened upon the attackers. Those men who survived the first fusilade tumbled out of the boats into about four feet of water. Many more were hit in the water and a number were drowned, pulled down by their heavy packs. Nevertheless, with their rifles soaked, and amid great confusion, the survivors pushed forward and began to force their way through and under the wire. C Company, under Captain R. R. Willis, emerged in some sort of formation and began to scale their company objective, Hill 114. Meanwhile D Company, under Major G. S. Adams, which had embarked in *Implacable*, had altered course to some rocks on the left of the beach. They scaled the cliff and completely surprised the Turks. They attacked and bayoneted the Turkish holders of the machine-gun nest which had been the main cause of the damage to the other companies. D Company was then able to enfilade the Turkish trenches facing W Beach.

In the water, entangled in the underwater wire, lay 300 Fusiliers who were either dead or severely wounded. In the actual landing operations sixty-three out of eighty naval ratings were killed or wounded. The brigadier was wounded and the brigade-major killed and eleven officers and 350 men of the Lancashire Fusiliers had become casualties.

On the extreme right the attack on Hill 138 by A Company under Lieutenant R. Haworth and B Company under Captain Shaw was struggling forward, when a naval shell failed to clear the top of the cliff and exploded, causing considerable confusion and a number of casualties. Haworth was wounded in the back but remained on duty.

By 7.15 am some sort of position had been established, sufficient to protect the beach from aimed fire. As the afternoon wore on and Turkish reinforcements were thrown into the counter-attack the Worcesters from the 88th Brigade, who were advancing from X Beach with a party of the Fusiliers under Captain Tallents, who carried on in spite of being badly wounded, recaptured Hill 114 and took a number of Turkish prisoners. W Beach was then firmly in British hands.

The Lancashire Fusiliers had certainly covered themselves with glory and the Divisional Commander asked their commanding officer, Major Bishop, to submit six names for the Victoria Cross. They were Captain R. R. Willis, Sergeant A. Richards, Captain C. Bromley, Private W. Keneally (posthumous), Lance Corporal J. Grimshaw and

Sergeant F. E. Stubbs (posthumous). All these were selected by their comrades and all six received the award.

Perhaps the outstanding character of this wonderful feat of arms was Cuthbert Bromley. He was thirty-seven when he won his Cross – unusually old. He was educated at St Paul's School and was commissioned in the Lancashire Fusiliers in 1898 when he was twenty years old. In 1914 he became Adjutant of the 1st Battalion. During his service with the regiment in India he had established a reputation as a leader, both in work and in sport: it was only indomitable leadership which could have pressed the shattered remnants on to their objective at Gallipoli on 25 April 1915. He had been wounded twice and was not fully recovered before he was given command of the battalion. Then, on 28 June, the battalion was ordered to attack across the open in broad daylight. The attack failed with heavy casualties and Bromley was wounded and sent back to hospital in Alexandria. He constantly begged to be allowed to return to his battalion in Gallipoli and he was sent back in the *Royal Edward*. She was torpedoed and Bromley went down with the ship. They don't come more gallant than that.

Even more ghastly scenes of carnage occurred at V Beach, near the ruined fort of Sedd-el-Bahr. This was a smaller beach than W and even more strongly defended. An important part of the plan for this landing centred round the converted collier *River Clyde* under command of Commander Unwin, R N, from which a living freight of some 2000 men was to be put ashore. They came from the 1st Royal Dublin Fusiliers, the 1st Royal Munster Fusiliers, the 2nd Hampshire Regiment, the West Riding Field Company of Royal Engineers and part of the Anson Battalion, Royal Naval Division. Four sally-ports had been cut in the collier, two to each side at lower deck level, where the men would be waiting to disembark. The sally-ports opened on to a gangway which led forward to the bows, where there was a hinged extension which led on to a motor hopper, the *Argyle,* backed up if necessary by lighters which were to bridge the gap between the *River Clyde* and the beach. By this method it was hoped to empty the ship within a few minutes. Machine-guns were mounted behind sandbags in the bows and on the deck to keep the Turk's heads down whilst the landing was taking place. It was considered that the enemy's defences could be shattered by the same preliminary bombardment as was shelling W Beach.

The first echelon of the assault was to disembark, not from the *River Clyde*, but from six tows of boats carrying 500 men of the 1st Royal Dublin Fusiliers and fifty men from the Anson Battalion. The *River Clyde* was to follow this covering echelon. In actual fact, owing to certain unforeseen delays, both the covering force in the boats and the *River Clyde* touched down almost together.

The *River Clyde* with the *Argyle* and two lighters in tow had started on her perilous mission at 10 pm on 23 April and had anchored that night at Tenedos. At 4 pm on the twenty-fourth the 2000 troops came aboard and they started their final approach at midnight. Then came the naval bombardment of V Beach, after which Commander Unwin went in to the beach with three tows of the covering force on one side of him and three on the other.

The Turks had retired under cover during the ships' bombardment and crept quietly back to their positions when it ceased. There were only three platoons of them and four machine-guns. They held their fire until the last moment and then opened a murderous blaze of musketry on the boats of the covering force. The carnage and damage inflicted was appalling. In a few minutes nearly every man was a casualty and the boats were riddled with bullets. In spite of their losses, however, a few officers and men managed to get ashore.

Meanwhile *River Clyde* had beached but owing to a miscarriage of the plan for the operation of the *Argyle* there was an unbridged gap between ship and shore. It was then 7.05 am and all surprise had disappeared as the Munsters, followed by the Dublin Fusiliers and the Hampshires, attempted to launch themselves from the belly of the *River Clyde* into a hail of fire. The lighters and the *Argyle* became a shambles and soon attempts to land were stopped. The few men who had got ashore found a position sheltered from the enemy's fire at the far end of the beach. The cries of the wounded in the lighters and in the water were heart-rending.

Prodigies of valour were performed on this day in bridging the gap, getting some of the men ashore and rescuing some of the wounded. Six Victoria Crosses were won in this desperate action on V Beach on 25 April. First and foremost was that of Commander Unwin, who had been the man in charge. He was over fifty years of age and showed incredible endurance and courage in maintaining the shifting bridge with the beach, in getting men ashore, and in keeping up the morale of the troops, both naval and military, in a situation where every single factor was loaded heavily against them and there appeared to be no end to the death and destruction they had to endure. He risked his life so many times that it was perhaps only right that God should have ordained that he should keep it. Unwin was greatly assisted by five other gallant sailors, all of whom won the Victoria Cross and of whom Sub-Lieutenant A. W. St C. Tisdall and Able Seaman W. C. Williams were posthumous. Of the others, Midshipman George Drewry had been in charge of the *Argyle* with Able Seaman Samson who had been wounded several times and remained with the lighter the whole day, and Midshipman Wilfred St Aubyn Malleson, who had been Commander Unwin's chief assistant throughout a very ghastly day.

General Hunter-Weston, the 29th Divisional Commander, had issued orders that the main body of the 88th Brigade, under command of Brigadier-General H. E. Napier, was to wait off V Beach in the *Clacton* until the boats of the covering force had returned, when they were to be taken over to the *River Clyde* and put ashore there. But owing to the almost complete destruction of the tows there were only sufficient boats left to accommodate the brigadier-general and his staff, fifty men of the Hampshires and two platoons of the Worcesters. Napier duly arrived and sprang on board the *Argyle*, not realizing that all the men on the hooper and the lighters were dead. He was determined to land and take charge of the men who had got ashore, but he was immediately shot down and killed.

Lieutenant-Colonel C. H. M. Doughty-Wylie, CB, CMG, of the Royal Welch Fusiliers was on the Headquarters Staff of the Mediterranean Expeditionary Force. As he knew the Turks and had been attached to the Turkish Army during the Balkan Wars, he had obtained permission from Sir Ian Hamilton to join the *River Clyde* party. During the day of 25 April Doughty-Wylie was a tower of strength, assisting the wounded and encouraging the men. On the death of General Napier he became the senior officer.

After dark, when the men remaining in the *River Clyde* were able to get ashore, he landed with them, taking with him Captain G. N. Walford, Brigade-Major 29th Divisional Artillery. Next morning, with magnificent gallantry, Doughty-Wylie rallied the somewhat battered survivors and led them forward. Fortunately, at the same time the naval ships began a heavy bombardment of the Old Fort and the village of Sedd-el-Bahr which the Turks were holding and this assisted and encouraged them greatly. After clearing the village of Sedd-el-Bahr he led a bayonet charge up to Hill 141, which had been their final objective. In the hour of victory both Doughty-Wylie and Captain Walford were killed and both were awarded posthumous vcs. Hill 141 was afterwards named 'Doughty-Wylie Redoubt'. Corporal William Cosgrove of the 1st Battalion Royal Munster Fusiliers was also awarded the vc on this day.

There has probably never been an operation in which the Navy and the Army have worked together with such self-sacrifice and so much gallantry in such terrible circumstances. The Anzacs (Australian and New Zealand Corps), 30,000 strong, comprised nearly half the infantry at Sir Ian Hamilton's disposal. They were grand men, tall, lithe and strong, and brave as lions. They were to make a great reputation in Gallipoli and Anzac Day was for ever after celebrated, both in Australia and London. Their beloved and celebrated commander, General Birdwood (late Field-Marshal Lord) became a legendary figure. He was known always as 'Birdie' and was often referred to as 'the Soul of Anzac'.

While the Royal Naval Division steamed on throughout the night of 24/25 April, to launch a diversionary attack on Bulair, the Anzacs were transferred from their transports to the three battleships which were to take them to within a couple of miles of the shore. There, soon after 2 am on the morning of 25 April, they were transferred again to cutters which were taken in tow by pinnaces to within rowing distance of the beaches. Their landing surprised the Turks and, had it not been for Mustapha Kemal, the celebrated Turkish commander, who organized a powerful counter-attack, the Anzacs might well have captured the commanding heights which would have struck a fatal blow at the heart of the Turkish defences of Gallipoli.

Between 19 May and the end of August 1915, eighteen vcs were won in Gallipoli and the Dardanelles. Of these the Royal Navy won one, British units seven, Australians nine, and New Zealanders one.

It was in the grim little battle of Lone Pine on 8/9 August 1915 that the Australians won seven of their nine vcs. The attack was launched by the 1st Australian Brigade (1st, 2nd, 3rd and 4th Battalions), later reinforced by the 12th and 7th Battalions, commanded by Brigadier-General Nevill Maskeline Smyth, VC, who had won his Cross at Khartoum in the Sudan on 2 September 1898. The British High Command realized that the Turks regarded the Lone Pine position as one of the main points in their defensive system and were confident that they would fight strongly to defend it. That was the object of the exercise – to keep the Turks pinned down at Lone Pine and prevent them sending reinforcements to Sari Bair, against which the main Anzac attack was to be made. But the 1st Australian Brigade went one better; in a bitter struggle lasting four days they established themselves so firmly in the Lone Pine entrenched position that not all the reinforcements which the Turks threw in there succeeded in dislodging them.

The highly built-up parapet of the Turkish front line stood out clearly above the sparse low scrub which separated the two trench systems. The Australian plan was to make their assault with three battalions, the 2nd on the right, the 3rd in the centre and the 4th on the left, with the 1st Battalion in reserve. To destroy the Turkish wire and break down their strong headcover a preliminary bombardment was staged lasting three days. This was of course nothing like the shattering bombardments known later in France – there were neither the guns nor the ammunition in Gallipoli – but by the afternoon of 6 August most of the Turkish wire had been destroyed.

At 5.27 pm the whistles blew to signal the start of this very desperate and heroic adventure. The leading companies of the two left assaulting battalions were soon into the Turkish forward trench. Only a line of Australian dead on the right showed that part of the 2nd Battalion had been caught in the open by a machine-gun. Behind the Turkish forward trench line there was a system of support trenches, communication trenches and tunnels. The Australian attack had come upon the Turks too quickly to allow them to man all their defensive positions but they now counter-attacked with the greatest determination.

The fighting was largely hand-to-hand within the trench system, with bomb and bayonet, and the most dangerous and effective Turkish weapon was the hand-grenade. The Australians were eager to reply in kind but were not only short of bombs but bomb throwers. By early morning of the seventh the bomb factory near the beach had sent for-

51

ward all the grenades they had. The 'Mills' Grenade, which became so familiar to the troops in France, was not available in Gallipoli. Jam tins were used as casings, filled with explosives and pieces of jagged metal. The Turkish bombs were cast-iron missiles, about the shape and size of a cricket ball. Both types of bomb had to be lit by a fuse before throwing.

The first Australian VC was won on 7/8 August by Private Keyzor of the 1st Battalion. He was an expert in both types of bomb and not only threw his own but picked up two Turkish bombs and hurled them back. Although he was wounded on the seventh he was in action next day and was wounded again.

Hectic hand-to-hand fighting continued day and night. The Turks were so anxious to retain Lone Pine that they flung reinforcements into the battle company by company as they arrived. The trenches captured by the Australian 2nd and 1st Battalions were literally floored with dead bodies. In the centre sector, however, which at dawn on the eighth was largely held by survivors of the 3rd Battalion, the strain had become so great that one of the forward trenches had to be abandoned.

A great effort had to be made to clear the trenches of the dead and during the remainder of the fighting this unpleasant, but most necessary, task was performed by the 5th Connaught Rangers.

On 9 August, the fourth and last day of the struggle for the Pine, the Turks made a final desperate attempt to drive the Australians out. Starting at 4 am under intensive covering fire they launched a violent attack. Encouraged by their officers, the Turks pressed forward along every trench. The Australians replied with everything they had, the officers using their revolvers. This was the fiercest fighting of all and on this day six VCs were won, four by the 7th Battalion – 2nd Lieutenant W. J. Symons, Captain F. H. Tubb, Corporal W. Dunston and Corporal A. S. Burton, the latter being posthumous ; one VC by the 1st Battalion – Captain A. J. Short, also posthumous ; and one by the 3rd Battalion – Private J. Hamilton.

The entire garrison of Captain Jacob's trench was caught in enfilade by a Turkish machine-gun and killed to a man. Early on the morning of the ninth Nevill Smyth put in his last reserve companies. That night the Turkish counter-attack was finally halted.

The four days fighting had cost the Australians over 2000 men, including eighty officers. Two of the commanding officers were killed and another severely wounded. In the 3rd Battalion every officer was hit except the quartermaster, including the medical officer and the chaplain. The enemy's losses were much heavier and the Turkish 16th Division was said to have lost 6,930 men.

Once again the Australians had proved themselves to be magnificent fighting men. The Battle of Lone Pine became an epic in Australian military history and will always be remembered with pride.

No story of the Dardanelles would be complete without some mention of Lieutenant Norman Holbrook, R N's exploit in command of Sub-marine *B 11*, which won him the award of the VC for sinking the Turkish battleship *Messudiyeh* on 13 December 1914. As the first submarine ever to torpedo a battleship, the *B 11* and her gallant commander deserve a special niche in the history of naval warfare. *B 11* belonged to one of the oldest groups of British submarines, having been launched in 1905.

On 13 December 1914 she was lying off the Dardanelles when Holbrook was ordered to attempt the passage of the Dardanelles and do what damage he could before returning. Lieutenant Holbrook was informed that there was a Turkish battleship lying to the north of Chanak, which was to be his particular target. He was also informed that the Straits were protected by a minefield consisting of five rows of mines extending across the width of the channel. In addition to the minefields and other obstructions, by which the Straits were defended, the natural difficulties of navigation were extremely threatening. There was a current running from the Sea of Marmora to the Mediterranean, often at a rate of five knots. The passage through the Straits was likely, therefore, to be very slow as *B 11* would be unable to proceed at a greater speed than six knots when submerged. The project was considered to be so hazardous that everyone on board the submarine left a farewell letter to be posted if the writers never returned.

At 3 am on 13 December *B 11* left her parent ship. Proceeding at first on the surface, she later submerged until, at a depth of sixty feet, she crept, blind, along the treacherous passage, risking rocks and shoals. In this fashion she passed under the minefields. As soon as she entered the Sea of Marmora she raised her periscope and at once spotted the battleship. At periscope depth the *B 11* closed with her target and her first torpedo struck the *Messudiyeh* a mortal blow and she was seen to be sinking by the stern.

At once enemy forts and destroyers spotted the submarine's periscope and opened fire furiously. *B 11* submerged quickly and headed for the Straits, pursued so closely by enemy destroyers that she was compelled to remain submerged for nine hours. At last, when all was clear, she completed the voyage back to her parent ship safely. It had been a very perilous adventure.

10

Eight VCs awarded to Indian Army Units in France, 1914-15.

In the period of about a year in which the Indian Corps fought in France, the eighteen Indian battalions were awarded only eight Victoria Crosses, which went to three British officers and five Indian ranks. The arrival of the Indian Corps in France in September 1914 was most opportune as the original British Expeditionary Force, the Old Contemptibles, were being bled to death and had been stretched to the limit in the early operations, most particularly in the bloody First Battle of Ypres which started at the end of October 1914. It was here that the Germans made their tremendous effort to finish off the Old Contemptibles for good and all; when, after ten days of savage fighting, Kaiser Wilhelm II arrived at Ypres and threw in the renowned Prussian Guard in a last do-or-die assault, it appeared that only a miracle could save the British. But they stood firm and by 20 November the Germans seemed to have shot their bolt; as the last attack petered out the British troops started cheering and the cheering gradually spread along the whole length of the British line in a roaring crescendo of sound.

Meanwhile the Indian Corps had started to arrive in Marseilles. It had been arranged that the Lahore and the Meerut Divisions should have a period of six weeks intensive training to accustom them to western conditions. The situation was much too critical for that, however, so that formations and even units of the Indian Corps had to be flung into the line wherever the need was greatest. My own unit, the 15th Ludhiana Sikhs, went into action on my twenty-first birthday, 24 October 1914, and on 31 October, at Hollebeke, the first Indian VC of the war was won by Sepoy Khudadad Khan of the 129th Duke of

Connaught's Own Baluchis. Khudadad Khan, though a sepoy in a Baluch regiment, was actually a Pathan. The 127th, 129th and the 130th Baluchi Regiments were mainly recruited from Mohammedans of various tribes on the north-west frontier of India.

Each of the six brigades in the Lahore and Meerut Divisions of the Indian Corps consisted of one British and three Indian battalions. Each Indian battalion had an establishment of twelve British officers, who formed the steel framework, as it were, of an Indian unit, and some twenty Indian, or viceroy's commissioned officers. The chief difficulty under which Indian units laboured in this western theatre of war was the severe nature of the casualties and the supply of reinforcements. A British officer reinforcement was of no use to an Indian unit unless he could speak the language of his men. This meant that whereas a British unit could get its casualties replaced within weeks by reinforcements from England, the Indian battalion had to wait months and in the meantime had to take over trenches held by a British battalion of twice its strength. Bearing in mind these handicaps and also of course the extremely difficult one of rations, the Indian troops put up an amazing performance in France at a critical period of the war. The martial races of India were natural and hereditary soldiers and they gave fine proof of this when they were needed most.

Sepoy Khudadad Khan was in charge of one of the two guns in the machine-gun section. The British officer in charge of the detachment was wounded and the other gun was knocked out by a shell. Khudadad Khan, though wounded, remained working his gun after the other five men of the detachment had been killed. He was left by the enemy for dead but later managed to crawl away and rejoin his unit. The losses of the 129th Baluchis on that day were seven British officers killed or wounded, five Indian officers killed or wounded, 164 other ranks killed or wounded and sixty-four missing, of whom the majority were probably killed.

A month later the King, on his first visit to the battle front, presented Sepoy Khudadad Khan with his Cross while he was recovering from his wounds in a field hospital.

The second Indian soldier to receive the VC was Naik (Corporal) Darwan Singh Negi of the 1st Battalion 39th Garhwal Rifles for his bravery at Festubert on the night of 23/24 November 1914. The

Garhwali is one of the finest natural soldiers I have ever known, like the Gurkha whom he closely resembles. Both are hillmen, Garhwal lying east of Nepal which is the home of the Gurkhas. On this occasion the 1/39th were ordered to retake some trenches which had just been captured by the Germans. The 1/39th took them by working along the trenches from the flanks. They captured 100 German prisoners, two machine-guns, one trench mortar, over 100 rifles and bayonets and much equipment, killed thirty-two Germans and wounded six more.

In the whole of this very dangerous and successful operation Naik Darwan Singh Negi was the first to pass round every traverse. He was wounded in the arm and in the head, but he kept advancing. King George V sent for this gallant Naik and presented him with his Cross at GHQ in France.

Lieutenant Frank de Pass, 34th Prince Albert Victor's Own Poona Horse, was the first British officer of the Indian Army to win the Victoria Cross in France – near Festubert on 24 November 1914, at the age of twenty-seven. He had been commissioned in the Royal Field Artillery in 1906 and in 1909 transferred to the Poona Horse. His decoration was won for entering a German sap and destroying a traverse in the face of enemy bombs and subsequently rescuing under heavy fire a wounded sepoy of the 58th Rifles. He then attempted to recapture the sap-head which the Germans had again reoccupied, but was shot through the head and killed.

Lieutenant William Bruce, 59th Scinde Rifles, also won a posthumous VC near Givenchy on 19 December 1914. During a night attack he was in command of a small party which captured one of the enemy trenches. In spite of being severely wounded in the neck he walked up and down the trench encouraging his men to hold on against enemy counter-attacks. It was owing to his great leadership and skilful dispositions that his men resisted for so long but they were at last overwhelmed by the Germans and the gallant Lieutenant Bruce was killed.

Rifleman Gobar Singh Negi of the 2nd Battalion 39th Garhwal Rifles, won his VC at the battle of Neuve Chapelle on 10 March 1915. It was a great achievement for one Indian regiment of two battalions to have won two of the only eight VCs awarded to the Indian Army in France.

Jemadar Mir Dast, IOM, of the 55th Coke's Rifles (FF), attached 57th

57

Wilde's Rifles, won the next Indian Army vc at Ypres (Belgium) on 26 April 1915 when he led his platoon with great gallantry during an attack. When all the British officers had become casualties he collected various parties of the regiment and kept them under his command until a retirement was ordered. This brief citation conceals a very historic occasion, not only for the Indian Army, but for the British Forces in France. It was the first use of gas which, if the Germans had only realized its devastating effect on totally unprotected troops, might well have won them the war.

The poison gas used was chlorine, discharged from cylinders previously established in the front line trenches. It was first used on 22 April in the Ypres Salient against a French division. Its effect was electrifying and the division fled in terror; its effect on the Lahore Division, which was called upon to counter-attack a few days later, was equally alarming as they knew what they were up against and were equally unprotected. When this crisis occurred the Lahore Division – in which I was a lieutenant in the 15th Sikhs in the Sirhind Brigade of that division – was holding a line of trenches at Festubert on the extreme right of the British Army. We had been in the front line for a week in trenches over a foot deep in mud and water. The condition of the men's feet may be imagined. Suddenly we received orders that we were to be relieved that night and proceed immediately by forced marches to Ypres. The distance was thirty miles, behind the whole of the British front, and the weather had suddenly turned very hot and our wet boots dried like boards. During that first year of the war in France Indian troops were called upon to undertake many hazardous operations, but never one so unpleasant and dangerous as this. We could not help wondering whether perhaps some division which had not been in the front line at the time could not have done this job which we were called upon to undertake.

As we passed through Corps HQ the division formed single file and every man had to dip his handkerchief into buckets which were supposed to contain some sort of anti-gas preparation. The hot sun, however, dried the handkerchiefs long before we got to Ypres, so that we never knew whether it would have had any effect or not.

Meanwhile the Germans had contented themselves with consolidating the ground they had gained. They had reversed the captured

trenches and wired them strongly. The three brigades of the Lahore
Division were in their assembly positions by 11 am on the twenty-sixth.
After a short and necessarily very inadequate artillery bombardment
the attack commenced at 2 pm. The Sirhind Brigade was in divisional
reserve so that I climbed up on top of a flat-roofed house to watch the
progress of the attack.

Despite an inferno of fire from the enemy guns and machine-guns
the attack was proceeding steadily and well until from the German
trenches issued a cloud of heavy greenish-yellow vapour which rolled
slowly over the attacking troops. It left behind a scene of complete
confusion. Men were running blindly, some sideways, some forwards
and some backwards, trying to escape from this dreadful choking death.
It was apparent to me at once that the attack must fail with ghastly
casualties. The losses in the 47th Sikhs were nine British officers, eight
Indian officers and 331 other ranks – or seventy-eight per cent of the
battalion.

The attack of the Ferozepore Brigade, on the left of the Jullunder
Brigade, suffered much the same fate. The 57th Rifles, Mir Dast's regiment, lost their commanding officer and soon were left with only two
British officers. When the battalion was thrown back in confusion
Jemadar Mir Dast remained behind in a trench after his officers had
been killed or wounded. He rallied all the men he could find, amongst
them some who had been only slightly gassed and were starting to recover. He held on to his position until he was ordered to retire after
dusk. During his retirement he collected a number of men from various
trenches and brought them in. Subsequently he assisted in bringing in
eight wounded British and Indian officers, being himself wounded in
doing so.

Few men who swallowed chlorine gas ever fully recovered and Mir
Dast, promoted to subadar, was no exception. His gas poisoning became
more marked and he was retired from the Service two years later.

I was so appalled by what I saw from my roof top and so rivetted to
the scene, that I did not notice that little swirls of gas were drifting
round me. As I was called down with the news that the 15th Sikhs and
4th Gurkhas were to make a night attack, I got a whiff of chlorine
which affected me for many years afterwards.

Then followed my own VC at Richebourg L'Avoué on 18 May 1915

- that little cockpit of the Western Front which the troops called the 'Glory Hole'. I was the only survivor of my small bombing party and the only British officer of the Indian Army to win the Cross in France in 1915.

The last of the eight Indian Army vcs was Rifleman Kulbir Thapa, 2nd Battalion 3rd Gurkha Rifles, at Fauquissart on 25 September 1915. When he had been wounded in an attack he found a badly wounded soldier of the 2nd Leicestershire Regiment behind the first line German trench, and although urged by the British soldier to save himself, he remained with him for the rest of that day and all night. In the early morning of the twenty-sixth, in misty weather, he brought him through the German wire and, leaving him in a place of comparative safety, brought in two wounded Gurkhas. He then went back in broad daylight for the British soldier and succeeded in carrying him in on his back, being at most points under enemy fire. The book, *With the Indian Corps in France*, describes Kulbir Thapa's action as:

'A deed which could hardly be surpassed for sheer bravery. Kulbir succeeded, after being wounded, in getting through the wire in some extraordinary way and charged straight through the German trenches.'

Kulbir Thapa recovered from his wounds and returned to India with his regiment.

11

Mesopotamia.

Twenty-two Victoria Crosses were awarded in the Mesopotamia Campaign, one in 1915, twelve in 1916 and nine in 1917. The terrain in which this campaign was fought could be described in a few words as a dead level plain, a desert of sun-baked alluvial soil, through which flowed the Euphrates and Tigris rivers, both uniting at Kurnah to form the Shatt-el-Arab, which then flowed on for roughly a hundred miles into the Persian Gulf. It was a country of sand, mud, mirage and blazing heat in the hot season. The only greenery to be seen anywhere was along the banks of the rivers which were bordered by large and valuable date palm groves varying in breadth from 200 yards to two miles in the vicinity of Basra. Beyond this belt on either side stretched the desert.

It was not an attractive theatre of war to the British and Indian soldiers, the former describing it in almost unprintable, but most descriptive, terms. Also the Turk, as was found in Gallipoli, was a very tough fighter. From the time the operations started the Navy gave the troops all possible support and in the early stages of the advance excellent work was done by small sloops armed with 4-inch and 3-pounder guns. Paddle steamers, too, and every sort of river craft were brought into service.

The first Mesopotamia vc was awarded posthumously to Lieutenant-Commander Edgar Cookson, DSO, RN, for his gallantry during the advance on Kut-el-Amara on 28 September 1915. Cookson had already won a DSO on 9 May for conducting a reconnaissance up a creek of the Euphrates in the Launch *Shushan*. He was severely wounded in this action but managed to extricate his vessel from a perilous position.

After a short spell of rest to recover from his wounds Cookson was appointed to command the *Comet,* one of the largest vessels of the river flotilla. *Comet* had been ordered, with other gunboats, to examine, and if possible destroy, an obstruction placed across the river by the Turks. When the gunboats approached the obstruction very heavy rifle and machine-gun fire was opened upon them from both banks. An attempt to sink the centre dhow of the obstruction having failed, Lieutenant-Commander Cookson ordered the *Comet* to be placed alongside and himself jumped on to the dhow and tried to cut the wire hawsers connecting it with the other two craft forming the obstruction. He was immediately shot and killed.

The first three vcs of 1916 were won by the Indian Army: the first by Sepoy Chatta Singh of the 9th Bhopal Infantry at the battle of the Wadi on 13 January. When the battalion's attack was repulsed a number of wounded men were left lying in the open, including the commanding officer, Colonel Thomas. Under heavy fire Chatta Singh went out to assist him. He bound his wound, dug some cover for him with his entrenching tool and remained with him until nightfall when he obtained assistance and brought him in to safety. Colonel Thomas, however, died of his wounds.

Lance Naik Lala of the 41st Dogras and Captain John Sinton of the Indian Medical Service both won their vcs at Orah Ruins on 21 January. Captain Sinton, though shot through both arms and through the side, refused to go to hospital and remained attending to his duties under very heavy fire. He was an iron man, both physically and mentally.

Two more Royal Navy vcs were won on 24/25 April, both of them posthumously by Lieutenant Humphrey Firman, RN, and Lieutenant-Commander Charles Cowley, RNVR.

The Army Commander had decided that an attempt should be made to get through supplies to the starving and beleaguered garrison of Kut by running a ship up the River Tigris. The steamer *Julnar* was selected for the purpose and specially prepared and protected with armour plating. She was then loaded with 270 tons of stores. Volunteers were called for to take part in this desperate venture and two officers and eleven men were selected. The two officers were Lieutenant Firman to command, with Lieutenant-Commander Cowley as his assistant.

Every possible precaution was taken to keep this venture secret and to distract the enemy's attention elsewhere. At 8 pm on 24 April the *Julnar* left Falihiyah and her departure was covered by all the artillery and machine-gun fire that could be brought to bear in the hope of causing a diversion. But the river, of course, was closely watched and she was soon discovered and heavily shelled from very close range.

At 1 am on the twenty-fifth, General Townsend reported from Kut that she had not arrived and that at midnight a burst of heavy firing had been heard at Magasis, some eight and a half miles from Kut by river. There could be little doubt that the enterprise had failed and the next day the Air Service reported *Julnar* in the hands of the Turks at Magasis. Both Lieutenant Firman and Lieutenant-Commander Cowley, who had performed magnificent service throughout the campaign in command of the *Mejidieh,* were reported by the Turks as killed in action. The remainder of the gallant crew, including five wounded, were made prisoners of war. With the capture of *Jalnar* the last hope of relieving the garrison of Kut had gone.

Two vcs were gained by the 9th Battalion Royal Warwickshire Regiment in an action on the west bank of the River Hai (near Kut) on 25 January 1917. One was awarded posthumously to Lieutenant-Colonel Edward Henderson who was attached to the regiment from the 2nd Battalion Royal Staffordshire Regiment and was commanding the 9th; the second went to his Adjutant, Lieutenant Robert Phillips, who was attached to the 9th from the 13th Battalion Royal War-wickshire Regiment.

Colonel Henderson brought his battalion up to our two front line trenches which were under intense fire. His battalion suffered heavy casualties on the way. The enemy immediately made a heavy counter-attack which succeeded in penetrating the battalion front in several places. At this time of great crisis Colonel Henderson, although shot through the arm, jumped on to the parapet and led his battalion forward in a desperate counter-attack, cheering his men on through a hail of bullets. Again wounded he continued to lead his men until they finally captured the Turkish position with a fierce bayonet charge. He was wounded twice more, the last time mortally, and was lying out in the open until Lieutenant Phillips, who had closely supported his colonel throughout, went out under intense fire and brought him in. Colonel Henderson was too badly wounded to survive.

Five Victoria Crosses were awarded to the troops in Mesopotamia in February and early March 1917. One of these was won by an officer of the Indian Army, Major George Campbell Wheeler of the 2/9th Gurkha Rifles. At Shumrau on the River Tigris on 23 February this officer, together with one Gurkha officer and eight men, crossed the river and rushed the enemy's trench in face of heavy fire. Having obtained a footing on the far bank he was counter-attacked by a strong bombing party. Major Wheeler at once led a charge, receiving in the process a severe bayonet wound in the head. However, he managed to disperse the enemy and consolidated his position. His bold and determined action undoubtedly saved the situation.

Private Jack White of the 6th Battalion Royal Lancaster Regiment won his vc on 7/8 March in an operation on the Dialah River. He was a signaller and during the river crossing he saw the two pontoons ahead of him come under heavy fire with disastrous results. When his pontoon reached mid-stream, with every man except himself killed or wounded, he tied a telephone wire to the pontoon, jumped overboard and towed it ashore, thereby saving an officer's life and bringing to land the wounded and the rifles and equipment of all the men.

Captain Oswald Reid of the 2nd Battalion The Liverpool Regiment, won his vc just afterwards, on 8/10 March, also at the Dialah River. He had been wounded in France with the 4th Battalion in April 1915 and again in 1916. He was wounded for the third time in winning his vc. He had shown dauntless courage when, with a handful of men, he was cut off on the far side of the river owing to the sinking of the pontoons connecting him with the remainder of his battalion. He maintained his position for thirty hours against constant attacks and continued in control despite being wounded. It was greatly owing to his tenacity that the passage of the river was effected successfully next morning.

Lieutenant John Graham, 9th Battalion Argyll and Sutherland Highlanders, attached 136th Company Machine Gun Corps, and Private Charles Melvin, 2nd Battalion Royal Highlanders (The Black Watch), both won their vcs at Istabulat in April 1917.

Graham was operating with the 56th Rifles (Frontier Force) Indian Army. Although twice wounded in the advance he continued to control his machine-guns effectively. When his last remaining gun was put out of action and he was again wounded he brought a Lewis-gun into action with excellent results. He was again severely wounded and forced to retire but his valour and skill with his weapons held up a strong enemy counter-attack and saved a critical situation from developing, when the advance of his company was held up.

Private Charles Melvin rushed forward by himself and entered the Turkish trench after killing two men by rifle fire. He then attacked the enemy in the trench with his bayonet, killing two more and taking eight prisoner. Then, driving these eight men before him and supporting one that had been wounded, he delivered them over to an officer before rejoining his company. Throughout the day he had inspired his comrades with confidence and courage.

12

Jutland, 1916.

Jutland, on 31 May 1916, was the only great naval battle of the First World War and nothing approaching it has taken place since in European waters, nor is ever likely to do so. Admiral Jellicoe, of whom it was truly said that he was the only man who might have lost the war in twenty-four hours, had primarily to make a German victory impossible rather than to take undue risks to press home a decisive British advantage. The British losses were three battle cruisers, three cruisers and eight destroyers. The Germans lost one battleship, one battle cruiser, four light destroyers and five destroyers. The British casualties numbered 6,784 and the German losses were 3,039.

Considering the vast scale of the battle, the large number of ships engaged and the heroism displayed by so many British sailors of all ranks, the fact that only four vcs were awarded to the Fleet on this historic day does, I think, show beyond all question that the high standards of Britain's premier decoration for gallantry was being more than maintained by the Royal Navy.

Commander the Hon. Edward Barry Stewart Bingham, RN, was the third son of the fifth Baron Clanmorris. He joined the Navy in 1897 when he was sixteen. He was thirty-five when he won his vc.

At 4.15 in the afternoon of 31 May a division of destroyers, under Commander Bingham in *Nestor*, moved out towards the enemy with the object of delivering a torpedo attack. On the way they met a flotilla of enemy destroyers and a fierce fight took place in which two of the enemy's vessels were sunk. *Nestor*, *Nomad* and *Nicator* then attacked the enemy's battle cruisers under terrific fire. Finally Bingham sighted the enemy battle fleet and, followed by the one remaining destroyer of his division, *Nicator*, he closed in with dauntless courage to within 3000 yards of the enemy in order to attain a favourable position for firing his torpedoes. While making this attack *Nestor* and *Nicator* were under the concentrated fire of the secondary batteries of the High Seas Fleet. *Nestor* was sunk and Commander Bingham was picked up by the Germans.

Boy John Travers Cornwell of the light cruiser *Chester* was under sixteen and a half years old. He was mortally wounded in the first few minutes of the action but remained standing alone in a most exposed position by his gun, waiting for orders, with the gun crew dead or wounded round him. He was carried ashore and died two days later in Grimsby hospital. His action has often been quoted as a great example of devotion to duty.

Major Francis John William Harvey of the Royal Marine Light Infantry in HMS *Lion* was mortally wounded when an enemy shell exploded in a gunhouse. Nevertheless, before he died, with great presence of mind he ordered the magazine to be flooded, thereby saving the ship.

Commander Loftus William Jones in HMS *Shark*, a torpedo-boat destroyer, led a division of destroyers to attack the German battle-cruiser squadron. In the course of this attack a shell hit *Shark's* bridge, putting the steering gear out of order, and shortly afterwards another shell disabled the main engines, leaving the vessel helpless. The commander of one of the other destroyers offered assistance but was warned by Commander Jones not to run the almost certain risk of being sunk.

Meanwhile, *Shark's* forecastle gun, with its crew, had been blown away and the same fate befell the after gun and crew. Commander Jones personally assisted in keeping the mid-ship gun in action. All this time *Shark* was being subjected to the close fire of enemy light cruisers and destroyers. The gun's crew was reduced to three, of whom an able seaman was soon badly wounded. A few minutes later Commander Jones was hit by a shell splinter which took off his leg. He continued to direct the gun crew while a chief stoker improvized a tourniquet round his thigh. He gave orders that another ensign should be hoisted and then, seeing that his ship could not remain afloat much longer, he ordered the surviving members of the crew to put on life belts. Almost immediately *Shark* was struck by a torpedo and sunk.

Commander Jones was not among the few survivors who were picked up.

13

The Honourable
Artillery Company.

Two fine young officers, Reginald Leonard Haine and Alfred Oliver
Pollard, who had joined the Honourable Artillery Company together
in August 1914, were close friends at the time they both won the vc in
April 1917 in France and remained so all their lives.

The HAC was occupying a prominent salient in the British line while
being subjected to increasingly strong German attacks. Second Lieutenant Haine organized and led six bombing attacks against a strongpoint
which the Germans had established and which dangerously threatened
British communications. He captured the position, together with fifty
prisoners and two machine-guns. The enemy counter-attacked with a
battalion of the Guard and regained the position. Haine at once formed
a block in his trench and for the whole of the following night maintained his position against repeated determined attacks. Next morning
he reorganized his men and again attacked the strongpoint, pressing the
enemy back several hundred yards, and thus relieved the situation.

Throughout this very tough engagement Second Lieutenant Bill
Haine's superb courage, quick decision and sound judgement were
beyond praise. His vc was gazetted on 8 June 1917. For further acts of
gallantry he was awarded an MC and bar.

Second Lieutenant Alfred Oliver Pollard was a huge figure of a man
who had been awarded the Distinguished Conduct Medal at Ypres in
September 1915 and subsequently won the Military Cross and bar. For
these four gallantry awards – the vc, DSO, MC and bar – to be awarded to
one man was an almost unique occurrence.

At a critical stage in the operations described above Pollard, with only four men, counter-attacked with bombs, broke up the enemy's counter-attack and regained all the ground which had been lost. By his determination and dash, coupled with a complete contempt for danger he set a splendid example to his men.

14

The Tragedy of the Somme.

On this ghastly first day of the Somme battle, 1 July 1916, the British lost 60,000 men, of whom one-third were killed, and the only real success was some small penetration in the southern sector. Nine Victoria Crosses were won that day. The British Army's casualties on 1 July were the equivalent of seventy-five battalions. For every yard of the Allied frontage there were two British casualties. Books have been written about this battle and more will be written in years to come. The worst of it was that the men lost were the flower of British youth who came forward voluntarily and eagerly in answer to Lord Kitchener's appeal for 'The First Hundred Thousand'. A great many of them were boys below the minimum age of nineteen who lied about their age.

A particular attraction to the new recruits was that Kitchener had promised that those who joined together could serve together. There were, therefore, 'City Battalions' and 'Pals Battalions', each with a special *esprit de corps* of their own, and all these 'Chums' units and units with local interest encouraged others to join.

There were, of course, the regular battalions who had borne the heat and burden of the day and were now having to be brought up to strength. They had a prestige of their own and had the advantage, which attracted many young men, of having their new recruits trained quickly and in action at the front with a highly disciplined unit much earlier.

There were also the Territorials, who found themselves a poor third in competing with the Regular Army and Kitchener's Army for new recruits.

On 1 July 1976, the sixtieth anniversary of the Somme, some very hard things were said about Sir Douglas Haig, the Commander-in-Chief of the British Army in France, and General Sir Henry Rawlinson, the 4th Army Commander, concerned with the conduct of the battle. In all fairness to them the following facts must be stated. As far back as 5 March 1916 Haig had been urged by Joffre to stage a major offensive north of the Somme to ease the pressure on the French at Verdun, and indeed to boost the very shaky morale of the French Army. French forces were to co-operate with the British. Haig had been ordered by his own Government to conform as far as possible with Joffre in the planning and conduct of the battle. Haig pressed for more time, particularly in order to stage an adequate artillery programme on which the lives of his men would depend. It was well known that the German trench system on this part of the front was exceptionally strong, with well built dugouts and fronted by masses of wire. There were not enough guns per mile of the British attack frontage, nor was there enough time to flatten the defence system before the infantry attack was launched. He wanted the starting date postponed to 15 August. Joffre flew into a rage and shouted : 'The French Army will have ceased to exist if you do nothing until then.'

On 30 March 1916 Lord Kitchener, on a visit to General Rawlinson's headquarters in France, was strongly against making a big attack at this time and would have preferred that the British continue small offensives with a view solely to killing Germans. But he was overruled.

Haig's plan, in conformity with the French, was to make an all-out assault on an eighteen-mile front with eighteen divisions belonging to Allenby's 3rd Army and Rawlinson's 4th. The majority of the divisions were New Army volunteers and Territorials, grouped under Rawlinson. The attacking force was almost entirely composed of county regiments. There were no Guards, Australians, Canadians, New Zealanders, South Africans, and the Indian Corps had, of course, been withdrawn from the Western Front and sent to Mesopotamia. The attack was supported by 185 aircraft and 455 heavy guns and howitzers.

The preliminary bombardment lasted from 24 June until 1 July. Considerable destruction was done to the wire and the front line trenches but the Germans retired to their deep dugouts, leaving lookout sentries to inform them of the attack which was certainly coming. On some sections of the front the Germans evacuated their front line trenches entirely. The long bombardment was a terrible ordeal for them, water and feeding became difficult, the wounded could not be evacuated nor the dead buried and their artillery had a shattering time. In the end it was the German machine-guns, the queen of the defensive battlefield, which settled the issue within the first hour of the battle ; the British played into their hands by encumbering the leading assaulting infantry with sixty pounds or more in weight, so that their advance was so slow that the German machine-gunners could emerge from their dugouts and take a terrible toll before the attackers were half way across no-man's-land. By making zero hour 7.30 am the allies gave away any element of surprise, which a dawn attack might have provided.

At 7.30 the artillery barrage lifted from the German defence system – and at that moment the leading lines of British infantry should have been close behind it. The German wire, however, was not nearly so flattened as the troops had been led to suppose. The only good thing about the first day of the Somme was the incredible bravery of the young New Army volunteers.

By 8.30 am, of the eighty-four battalions totalling some 66,000 men which had attacked at 7.30, about one-third had reached their first objectives. Another third had gained vulnerable footholds in the German trenches and the rest had been practically wiped out. The tragedy was that the second wave went forward according to plan, even in the areas where the first attack had failed completely and they were going to certain death. In these set-piece trench warfare operations once an attack of this magnitude had started it was almost impossible to halt. Those battalions which managed to get into the German trenches were amazed by the scale and indestructability of the German dugouts.

The nine Victoria Crosses won on this historic but tragic day were Temporary Captain E. N. F. Bell, 9th Battalion Royal Inniskilling Fusiliers and Light Trench Warfare Battery (posthumous) ; Lieutenant G. St G. S. Cather, 9th Battalion Royal Irish Fusiliers (posthumous) ; Captain J. L. Green, RAMC and 1/5th Battalion Notts and Derby Regiment (TF) (The Sherwood Foresters) (posthumous) ; Temporary Major S. W. Loudoun-Shand, 10th Battalion Yorkshire Regiment (Green Howards) (posthumous) ; Private W. F. McFadzean, 14th Battalion Royal Irish Rifles (posthumous) ; Private R. Quigg, 12th Battalion Royal Irish Rifles ; Drummer W. P. Ritchie, 2nd Battalion The Seaforth Highlanders ; Corporal G. Sanders, 1/7th Battalion West Yorkshire Regiment, and Sergeant J. Y. Turnbull, 17th Battalion Highland Light Infantry (posthumous).

Captain Eric Norman Frankland Bell was in command of a mortar battery. When the front line of his battalion was held up by enfilading machine-gun fire he crept forward and shot the machine-gunner. Later, on three occasions when bombing parties which were clearing the enemy front line trenches were held up, he went forward alone and threw his bombs with great effect. When the Germans counter-attacked he stood on the parapet and used his rifle. He was killed rallying a party of men who had lost their officers. He had no known grave.

Lieutenant Geoffrey St George Shillington Cather had joined the Army in the University and Public Schools Corps in September 1914, obtaining his commission in the 9th Battalion Royal Irish Fusiliers in May 1915. He was Adjutant of the Regiment when the Somme battle started. From 7 pm until midnight he searched no-man's-land for three wounded men whom he found and brought in. Next morning he continued his search, giving water and encouragement to those others he found, and in so doing he was killed. He, too, had no known grave.

Captain John Leslie Green was commissioned in the Royal Army Medical Corps on the outbreak of war and had only recently been attached to the Sherwood Foresters. Although he had been wounded he went to the assistance of a wounded officer who was hanging on the enemy's wire, as were many others on a section of the front where the attack had been unsuccessful. Despite the heavy fire directed at him, he had nearly managed to get him safely under cover when he was killed.

Major Stewart Walter Loudoun-Shand had served throughout the Boer War and had at once offered his services when the First World War started. He was gazetted to the 10th Green Howards. He had been given a temporary majority when his colonel and two majors had been killed in action. On this first day of the Somme he was commanding a company. He had led them right up to the German trenches when they were held up by machine-gun fire. Loudoun-Shand leapt onto the parapet, helped his men over it and continued to wave them on until he fell mortally wounded. Even then he insisted on being propped up in the trench and continued to encourage his men until he died.

Private William Frederick McFadzean of the 14th Royal Irish Rifles sacrificed his own life to save his comrades when the safety pins fell out of two grenades which were being issued to the men in a crowded trench before the attack. Realizing what terrible casualties this accident would cause he threw himself on top of them. He was blown to pieces but only one other man was injured.

Private Robert Quigg joined the Army in 1914 in the 12th Royal Irish Rifles. On 1 July, when his battalion had experienced heavy casualties in its unsuccessful attack, he heard that his platoon officer was lying wounded in no-man's-land. He went out seven times to search for him under heavy fire, each time bringing back a wounded man, the last one being only a few yards from the German wire. Eventually his officer was found and brought safely back.

Drummer Walter Potter Ritchie was only sixteen when he joined the 2nd Battalion Seaforth Highlanders in 1908. In the 1 July 1914 attack, when his battalion had reached the enemy trench and was under heavy fire, with many of the officers casualties, he stood on the parapet and repeatedly sounded the charge on his bugle. Throughout the day he carried messages over ground swept by enemy fire.

Corporal George Sanders joined the West Yorkshire Regiment in November 1914. After his battalion had captured the enemy front line trench he became isolated with a party of thirty men, of whom he took charge. When they were attacked next morning he drove the enemy back and rescued some prisoners who had fallen into their hands. He held his position with the greatest courage until he was relieved thirty-six hours later. He was given a commission and promoted captain in December 1918. In April 1918 he was wounded and taken prisoner in the hard fighting at Kemmel Hill, where he was awarded the Military Cross.

Sergeant James Young Turnbull of the 17th Battalion Highland Light Infantry had captured a German post with his men and was then subjected to heavy counter-attacks, which continued all through the day. Although his party suffered a number of casualties Turnbull never wavered in his determination to retain his post, the loss of which would have been serious to his battalion. Finally, almost single-handed, he maintained his position. Later in the day he was killed whilst leading a bombing counter-attack.

One of the most celebrated VCs in our history, Captain (Temporary Lieutenant-Colonel) Adrian Carton de Wiart, DSO, of the 4th Dragoon Guards, attached 8th Battalion Gloucestershire Regiment, was also in the front line on the fateful 1 July and won his VC two days later when the Glosters, whom he was commanding most gallantly, captured the German strongly fortified area of La Boiselle. It was largely owing to his dauntless courage and inspiring example that a serious reverse was avoided. He displayed the utmost determination in forcing the attack home. After three other battalion commanders had become casualties he controlled their commands as well as his own and ensured that the ground won was retained. In organizing the captured position he exposed himself fearlessly to the enemy fire and seemed to bear a charmed life.

Carton de Wiart was a legendary figure. At the outbreak of the South African War in 1899 he joined up in the Middlesex Yeomanry (Duke of Cambridge's Hussars) and was twice wounded and received the Queen's Medal with three clasps. In 1901 he received a commission in the 4th Dragoon Guards. In 1914-15 he was in action with the Somaliland Camel Corps, during which he lost an eye. He was mentioned in despatches and awarded the DSO. Later he served in France, where he was severely wounded several times and lost his left arm at Zonnebeke. In spite of this he was back in action commanding the Glosters for the Somme battle. He was wounded eight times during the First World War, in which, in addition to the VC, he was awarded the CB, CMG, the *Croix d'Officier de l'Ordre de la Couronne* and the *Croix de Guerre*. He commanded the British Military Mission to Poland from 1918 to 1924 and afterwards spent much time in that country.

When the Second World War broke out he volunteered for active service immediately, despite the fact that he was nearly sixty, and very shot about. He was given command of the Central Norwegian Expeditionary Force, was taken prisoner in 1941 and released in 1943. He was then sent to China as Winston Churchill's special military representative with Generalissimo Chiang-Kai-Shek.

I had never met Carton de Wiart until the beginning of the Second World War when I was Chief Staff Officer to the 2nd London Division and on the point of taking command of a brigade for the operations in

France leading up to Dunkirk. Not to have met Carton de Wiart would have been to miss a unique experience. The fabulous figure with the black patch over the missing eye, the empty sleeve pinned close to his chest, the bristling little moustache and the fine row of medals, the impeccably turned out, erect, small figure, slim and hard as nails, was an inspiration to be with. No day was ever too long for him, no obstacle too big ; he had even plucked out his own eye when he found it was no longer of service to him. Truly this man's spirit burned like a flame in his battered body.

The Battle of the Somme has come to be regarded as the greatest single tragedy of British arms. Although all hope of a quick breakthrough had diminished with the disaster of 1 July, the Somme offensive continued at a lower tempo all through July and August and after. It is difficult to give an objective, as opposed to an emotional, answer to the question 'Was the Somme worth while ?' Judging by the small extent of ground gained at the cost of such appalling casualties, the answer would be a definite 'No', but judged by the long-term effects – the relief it afforded to Verdun, the boost it gave to the shaky morale of the French Army and the wearing down of the Germans – the answer might be different. General Ludendorff, the German Chief of Staff, said later : 'By the end of 1916 the German Army was fought to a standstill and was utterly worn out.' If the French had given in, it could have resulted in the loss of the war.

In the final reckoning it could be argued that, had it not been for the Somme the German Army might never have lost the war ; conversely, had it not been for the Somme the Allied Armies might have won it sooner.

It was not until November 1916 that the Somme battle ended. The total Allied casualties were 343,112 British and 143,072 French. Some experts believed that the German casualties were even higher. The criticism against Haig and Rawlinson was severe, chiefly for not stopping it when it was obvious that no breakthrough could be effected. The strongest critic of these two generals was Winston Churchill, though he became a considerable admirer of Douglas Haig later in the war.

The last vc of this long-drawn-out battle was awarded to a very famous New Zealander, Captain Bernard Freyberg, on 13 November. It was also the last vc awarded in 1916. He was born in London on 21

Above left Lt Gen. Sir Frederick Roberts (later Field–Marshal Earl Roberts). As a subaltern of the Bengal Artillery in the Indian Mutiny, 2 January 1858, he saved the Colours by cutting down two mutinous sepoys.

Above right Lt the Hon. F. H. S. Roberts, Lord Roberts' only son, won a posthumous vc at Colenso in the South African War, 15 December 1899.

Right Lt H. H. Gough, who won his vc in the Indian Mutiny on 25 February 1858, was an intrepid cavalry leader in the 19th Royal Hussars.

Above Lt J. R. M. Chard commanded the little post at Rorke's Drift, Zulu War, 23 January 1879, against the Undi Corps, when eleven VCs were won.

Below left Lt G. Bromhead commanded the small party of South Wales Borderers at Rorke's Drift, 23 January 1879, who won the record number of seven VCs awarded to one regiment in a single action.

Below right Rev. J. W. Adams, Bengal Civil Service, Afghan War, 22 December 1879, one of the only four civilians to win the Cross.

Subadar Khudada Khan, 129th Baluchis, Belgium, 31 October 1914, the first Indian soldier to win the VC in the First World War.

Lt Harold Woolley, 9th Battalion London Regiment, one of the four VCs won at Hill 60, Belgium, 21 April 1915.

Lt J. G. Smyth, 15th Ludhiana Sikhs, won the only VC awarded to a British officer of the Indian Corps in France in 1915, 18 May 1915.

Capt. A. Ball, Royal Flying Corps, one of the most remarkable young airmen of all time, won his VC for service in France, April–June 1917.

Above Capt. J. B. McCudden, Royal Flying Corps, a great fighter pilot who accounted for fifty-four enemy planes, won his VC in France, 1917–18.

Below left Gen. Carton de Wiart won his VC at the Somme. He lost his eye and a hand, and was wounded eight times.

Below right Capt. B. C. Freyberg won his VC in France on 13 November 1916 when commanding the Hood Battalion of the Royal Naval Division.

Lt-Commander G. B. Roope won the first VC of the Second World War in the *Glowworm* off Norway on 8 April 1940.

Leading Seaman J. J. Magennis won his VC at Johore Straits on 31 July 1945 for fixing mines to the bottom of Japanese cruiser *Takao*.

Commander A. C. C. Miers of the Submarine *Torbay* won his VC on 5 March 1942. Three other officers and twenty of his crew were also decorated.

Capt. C. H. Upham, New Zealand Military Forces, one of only three men to win a bar to his VC, Crete and N. Africa, 1941–2.

Above left Private R. Kelliher, 2/25th Australian Infantry Battalion, won his VC in the operations against Japanese marines in New Guinea on 13 September 1943.

Above right Major D. V. Currie, 29th Canadian Armoured Recce Regiment, won his VC in Normandy, 18/20 August 1944.

Below Wing Commander G. R. Gibson was the famous 'Dambuster', whose squadron inflicted grievous damage on the Möhne and Eder Dams, 16/17 May 1943.

Wing Commander G. L. Cheshire, probably the greatest bomber pilot of all time, won his vc for flying duties, 1940–44.

Major W. P. Sydney (Viscount De L'Isle), Grenadier Guards, won his vc at the Anzio beachhead, Italy, 7/8 February 1944.

Pilot Officer A. C. Mynarski, Royal Canadian Air Force, Cambria, 12 June 1944, whose self-sacrifice in a Lancaster aircraft cost him his life but saved the lives of his crew.

Capt. D. Jamieson, Royal Norfolk Regiment, for action in Normandy, 7/8 August 1944.

The author with (*right*) Rifleman Bhanbhagta Gurung, 2nd Gurkha Rifles, Burma, 5 March 1945, and (*left*) Lance Corporal Rambahadur Limbu, 10th Gurkha Rifles, Sarawak, 21 November 1965. Both were famous VCs.

Rear-Admiral Godfrey Place VC presents Lt-Col. Haine VC to Prince Philip at the VC and GC reunion dinner, 22 April 1976.

March 1889 but his father was a New Zealander, and he was brought up in New Zealand and was first commissioned as a second-lieutenant in the 6th Hauraki Regiment, New Zealand Military Forces. He later transferred to the British regular Army and became a company commander in the Hood Battalion of the Royal Naval Division in 1914 and from 1915 to 1917 commanded that Battalion. He took part in the operations on the Gallipoli Peninsula from the landing until the evacuation. On the night of 24/25 April 1915 he won a very gallant DSO when he swam ashore at night, alone, and lit flares on the beach to distract attention from the landing operations which were taking place elsewhere. He was several hours in the water before being picked up.

Freyberg was then transferred to France and there took part in the battles of the Somme, Arras, Bullecourt, the third battle of Ypres, Paschendaele, the first battle of the Lys and the Forest of Nieppe, the Battle of Hill 63 and Ploegsteert Wood, the fourth Battle of Ypres, the Battle of Ledingham, the second Battle of Lys and the crossing of the Scheldt and Dendre.

Freyberg was awarded the Victoria Cross on 13 November 1916 while commanding the Hood Battalion as a captain (Temporary Lieutenant-Colonel) for his brave and brilliant leadership of the battalion. He carried the initial attack straight through the German front-line system of trenches, by which time the battalion had become much disorganized. He then personally rallied and re-formed them, with men of various other units, and led them on to the successful assault of the second objective, capturing many prisoners. During this advance he was wounded twice but remained in command and held his very advanced position for the remainder of the day and throughout the night. When reinforced next morning he organized an attack on a strongly fortified village and personally led the assault, capturing the village and 500 prisoners. In this operation he was wounded again. Later in the afternoon Freyberg was wounded once more, this time severely, but he refused to leave his battalion until he had issued final instructions. His fearless and inspired leadership enabled the lodgement in the most advanced objective to be held, and on this strongpoint the line was eventually formed.

Wherever the fighting was thickest Freyberg was always to be found, leading and encouraging his troops. He gained a second bar to his DSO in the last five minutes of the war. He finished the First World War as a brigadier, VC, CMG, DSO (with two bars), a brevet-majority, brevet lieutenant-colonelcy and six mentions in despatches. He had been wounded nine times.

In the Second World War Freyberg greatly distinguished himself in command of the New Zealand Division, was again wounded and won a third bar to his DSO. He was created a KCB and KBE, was Governor-General of New Zealand from 1946 to 1952 and was created a baron in 1951.

15

Three Famous Fighter Pilots.

Lieutenant Albert Ball, 7th Battalion Notts and Derby Regiment (Sherwood Foresters) and Royal Flying Corps, won his posthumous Victoria Cross for flying services in France between 25 April and 6 May 1917. In the fierce fighting which occurred on the Western Front during this period twenty-two VCs were awarded, and the casualties alone were five times greater than in the whole of the forces engaged in the Crimea.

By this time the Royal Flying Corps had grown enormously and played a major role in the operations.

Captain Ball's official citation reads:

In this period (of only a fortnight) he took part in twenty-six combats in the air and destroyed eleven hostile aeroplanes, drove down two out of control and forced several more to land. In these combats Captain Ball, flying alone, on one occasion fought six hostile machines, twice he fought five, and once four. When leading two other British aeroplanes he attacked a German formation of eight. On each of these occasions he himself brought down at least one enemy plane. Several times his aeroplane was badly damaged, once so seriously that, but for the most delicate handling, his machine would have collapsed as nearly all the control wires had been shot away. On returning with a damaged machine he had always to be restrained from immediately going up in another. In all, Captain Ball has destroyed forty-three German aeroplanes, and one balloon and has always displayed most exceptional courage, determination and skill.

Forty-three German planes is likely to be a considerable understatement as Captain Ball was always reluctant to claim any but those which were seen to be completely destroyed. He was certainly one of the most remarkable and intrepid young airmen of his time and when he was killed, at the age of twenty, he had won more honours for bravery in action than any man of his age had ever achieved before. He was the first officer to receive the DSO three times and his other awards for gallantry were the Victoria Cross, the Military Cross, the Russian Order of St George and the Legion of Honour. He was mentioned in despatches many times and also in parliament. On his twentieth birthday he was presented with the honorary freedom of his native city, Nottingham.

Albert Ball joined up at the outbreak of war as a private in the 2/7th Sherwood Foresters. He was mad keen on flying and took every opportunity to do so. He was a religiously minded young man of the highest ideals and principles. While he was with the Sherwood Foresters he would get up at 3 am and motor from Luton to Hendon and back to learn to fly. As soon as he could he applied to join the Royal Flying Corps and became a dedicated fighter pilot. He fought for his home and his country with a song in his heart – and death in his hands. 'I always sing', he said, 'when I am up in the clouds. I am never afraid. I am looked after by God.'

Ball was indeed utterly fearless and imbued with only one idea – to engage the enemy in the air at any place, at any time and against any odds. During the early battles on the Somme he would often be in the air by 2.30 am, and keep flying until 9.30 at night. Although completely confident in himself he was a man of absolute humility and never sought fame. In ordinary life he was a quiet and retiring man, but in the air he was a killer. He was never reckless, however. He took immense trouble to make himself a super-efficient airman and a crack shot. He kept himself, his plane and his gun in perfect order. He was always superbly fit in mind and body; he knew he had to be to keep at the top and to stay alive.

From the time Ball joined the RFC until his death he spent most of his waking hours scanning the skies for enemy aircraft and although his flying life was short – only one year in all – he certainly lived a lifetime in that year and died as he would have wished – engaging superior numbers of the enemy. He was reported missing on 8 May 1917. It was afterwards discovered that he had been shot down by anti-aircraft fire when he had attacked three German machines, shot down two and drove off the third. The Germans buried him in the German cemetery at Annoeullin with the greatest respect and honour. Then, at the risk of his life, a German pilot crossed the lines to drop a cylinder reporting his death. There was a great *cameraderie* between the top air aces of Germany and Britain in the First World War.

Sir Hugh Trenchard, the head of the Royal Flying Corps and later Marshal of the RAF, described Albert Ball as: 'The most daring, skilful and successful fighter pilot the Royal Flying Corps has ever had.'

Captain William Avery Bishop, DSO, MC, Canadian Cavalry and Royal Flying Corps, won the Victoria Cross near Cambrai, France on 2 June 1917, at the age of twenty-three. He was born at Ontario, Canada, and was in his second year at the Royal Military College, Kingston, when the war started. He enlisted in the 4th Canadian Mounted Rifles and went overseas with them a few months later. In 1915 he transferred to the Royal Flying Corps as an observer and in 1917 became a fighter pilot.

'Billy' Bishop accounted for seventy-two enemy planes and two balloons. In one period of twelve days he shot down twenty-five enemy machines and five on his last day in action. Although he commanded his squadron with outstanding leadership, his best and most daring achievements were as a solo flyer. He was awarded the MC and the DSO in 1917 and also a bar to his DSO. His chief speciality was gunnery and he was an outstanding aerial marksman. He was also a remarkable tactician in the air and made an intensive study of the habits and tactics of his opponents. He had supreme confidence in himself and in his own invincibility and events certainly justified this attitude. He would seize any chance of swooping down on a column of German infantry or transport on a road and spraying them with machine-gun bullets.

The official citation of his VC in the *London Gazette* of 11 August 1917 reads as follows:

For most conspicuous bravery, determination and skill, Captain Bishop, who had been sent out to work independently, flew first of all to an enemy aerodrome; finding no machines about, he flew on to another aerodrome about three miles south-east, which was at least twelve miles the other side of the line. Seven machines, some with their engines running, were on the ground. He attacked these from about fifty feet. One of the machines got off the ground, but at a height of only sixty feet Captain Bishop fired fifteen rounds into it at very close range and it crashed to the ground. A second machine got up which he shot down into a tree. Two more machines then rose from the aerodrome. One of these he engaged at a height of 1000 feet, emptying the rest of his drum of ammunition into it. This machine crashed 300 yards from the aerodrome; after which Captain Bishop emptied a whole drum into a fourth machine and then turned for home. Four hostile scouts were about 1000 feet above him but they would not attack. His machine was very badly shot about by machine-gun fire from the ground.

By the end of the war he held the rank of Lieutenant-Colonel and had added the DFC and the French Legion of Honour and *Croix de Guerre* to his other decorations. He was one of the few famous fighter pilots of any nation in the First World War who lived to tell the tale.

In the Second World War he served with the Royal Canadian Air Force as a director of recruiting and attained the rank of Air-Marshal.

Second Lieutenant (temporary Captain) James Byford McCudden, DSO, MC, MM of the General List and Royal Flying Corps, won his VC for flying services in France during the latter part of 1917 and early 1918 and his citation in the London Gazette of 2 April 1918 reads as follows:

Captain McCudden has up to the present time accounted for fifty-four enemy aeroplanes. Of these forty-two have been definitely destroyed, nineteen of them on our side of the lines. And twelve of the fifty-four have been driven down out of control. On two occasions he has totally destroyed four two-seater enemy aeroplanes on the same day and on the last occasion all four machines were destroyed in the space of one hour and thirty minutes.

While in his present squadron he has participated in seventy-eight offensive patrols, and in nearly every case has been the leader. On at least thirty other occasions, whilst with the same squadron, he has crossed the lines alone, either in pursuit of or in quest of enemy aeroplanes.

On 3 December 1917, when leading his patrol, eight enemy aeroplanes were attacked between 2.30 pm and 3.50 pm. Of these two were shot down by McCudden. On the morning of the same day he left the ground at 10.50 and encountered four enemy aeroplanes, of which he shot two down.

On the 30 January 1918, he, single-handed, attacked five enemy scouts, as a result of which two were destroyed. On this occasion he only returned home when the enemy scouts had been driven far east, his Lewis gun ammunition was all finished and the belt of his Vickers gun had broken.

As a patrol leader he has at all times shown the utmost gallantry and skill, not only in the manner in which he has attacked and destroyed the enemy, but in the way he has, during several aerial fights, protected the newer members of his flight, thus keeping down the casualties to a minimum.

James McCudden was born on 28 March 1895 at Gillingham in Kent, the son of a quartermaster-sergeant in the Royal Engineers. He joined the RFC as a mechanic in May 1913. He was awarded the *Croix de Guerre* and the Military Medal in 1916. In the following January he was given a commission. On 16 February he won the MC, with a bar the following October. The DSO followed on 14 December 1917, with a bar on 3 January 1918.

McCudden and the crack German fighter pilot, Immelmann, were deadly rivals. They had three duels in the air with no decisive advantage to either. James McCudden was promoted temporary major in July 1918 and killed on leaving Marquiz to take over his new squadron. Into eighteen months he had crowded a lifetime of precarious and gallant adventure.

16

Commander Gordon Campbell and the 'Q' Ships.

The first Royal Navy VC of 1917 was won by Commander Gordon Campbell, DSO, on 17 February when in command of HMS Q5. His official citation merely stated: 'In recognition of his conspicuous gallantry, consummate coolness and skill in command of one of HM ships in action.' It was obvious that there was much more behind this cryptic statement, as indeed there was – the whole epic story of the 'Q' ships and their great gallantry in taking on the German U-boats at the height of their depredations against British shipping in the Atlantic.

The very impressive list of his honours and promotion could have told any acute observer that Commander Campbell had been engaged in ventures of great hazard and of the highest national importance. He was specially promoted to commander on 29 March 1916, passing over the heads of over 700 lieutenant-commanders, and when promoted to captain on 17 June 1917 he passed over the heads of 500 commanders. He received the DSO on 31 May 1916 and was decorated with the VC on 17 March 1917, gained a bar to his DSO on 27 July 1917 and a second bar on 2 November 1917. He also received the *Croix de Guerre* with palms and was an *Officier Legion d'Honneur*. Had German Intelligence been better informed they might have connected the loss of some of their submarines with some of Commander Campbell's decorations and promotions and arrived at some accurate conclusions.

Not only was Commander Campbell a very brave man, a strong disciplinarian and a very inspiring leader, but he paid the most meticulous attention to every detail of the task in which he was engaged. On one occasion he dressed one of his crew as a girl and placed him in a prominent position on deck to attract telescopic attention to his ship. On another occasion, when the 'panic party' left the ship he had a mock-up parrot in a cage for them to take with them. He never left anything to chance.

By reason of the fact that secrecy was so important in the anti-submarine campaign in the First World War the British people were never told at the time of the terrible menace posed by the German submarines, and therefore of the gallant actions of the 'mystery ships' which were brought into being to combat them. Enemy submarines threatened the very life-blood of Britain. It was a bitter war, fought by highly armed ships of the German Navy against unarmed merchant vessels. Very many of these ships' crews were either ruthlessly extermi-nated or left to their own fate to die of exposure, thirst or drowning. It was a skin game and in the course of time the 'Q' ships got under the skin of the menacing German U-boats and made them much more cautious and fearful in their attacks on merchant shipping.

The submarines became vulnerable to the 'Q' ships only when 'they came up to spout' and, as they could carry only a limited number of torpedoes, they had to surface and rely on their guns for the majority of their kills against unarmed merchantmen. Thus they gave a chance – and often a very fleeting one – to the captains and crews of the 'Q' ships to attack them. The operations of these gallant men on the 'Q' ships, often perforce 'unhonoured and unsung', surely deserve a place amongst 'the Valiant' of all time.

Owing to the fact that the German submarines concentrated their attacks on the shipping in the western approaches to the British Isles the greatest sphere of 'Q' ship operations was off the south-west coast of Ireland. A 'Q' ship's personnel consisted of every kind of seaman – in-cluding officers and men of the Royal Navy, both active and retired, Royal Naval Reserve and Royal Naval Voluntary Reserve and of the Merchant Navy – who were willing to risk their lives in a great and hazardous adventure. There were no heroics about this service; every man who volunteered had to be a highly disciplined expert in his own particular field. The price of failure was death.

It was in March 1915 that the Admiralty had selected the tramp steamer ss *Baralong* as a decoy. Built in 1901 she was of 4,192 tons, speed ten knots, armed with three 12-pounders and fitted with a single wireless aerial, which could excite no suspicion. Indeed, so skilfully was her armament concealed that she could lie in harbour, close to foreign ships, without revealing her true nature. For nearly six months she cruised around, steaming some 12,000 miles without once contacting a German submarine. Then, on 19 August, she at last had her chance.

On 17 August, in the area between the south-west coast of Ireland and the western end of the English Channel, eight British steamers had been sunk, including the White Star Line *Arabic*, by German U-boats. In the hope of finding one of them *Baralong*, on 19 August, was cruising about 100 miles south of Queenstown, steering in an easterly direction. She was disguised as a United States cargo ship, with the American colours painted on boards on her sides. These boards were made so that they could be hauled in, and the ensign staff fell away as soon as the ship went into action with the White Ensign hoisted.

At 3 pm *Baralong* picked up a wireless signal from a steamer which appeared to be manoeuvring somewhat strangely. *Baralong* therefore altered course towards her. A submarine was sighted about seven miles away, heading towards the steamer, which she was shelling. By this time the crew of the steamer, the Leyland line *Nicosian*, were rowing about in ship's boats. The submarine *(U 27)*, with a 22-pounder gun forward of the high conning-tower, and a similar gun aft, steered so as to come along *Nicosian*'s port side and towards the latter's boats.

As soon as the submarine was blanketed by *Nicosian*, *Baralong*, now roughly parallel with the other two craft, struck her American colours, hoisted the White Ensign and trained her guns ready for the moment when the submarine should show herself ahead of *Nicosian*'s bows. When that moment came *Baralong* opened fire on the *U 27* with her guns and with small-arms fire at a range of only 600 yards.

The *U 27* was completely surprised and the 'Q' ship's shells had penetrated the submarine on the water-line below the conning-tower before she could reply. The conning-tower went up in the air, panic-stricken Germans jumped into the sea and the submarine keeled over and sank. *Baralong*'s tactics could not have been more simple, or more effective. To the crew of the *Nicosian* their delivery seemed like a miracle. The ship had been badly holed by the submarine's shells but *Baralong* took her in tow and managed to get her safely to port at Avonmouth.

The captain of the *U 27* was one of Germany's most highly regarded submarine commanders and it had left Germany only a fortnight earlier. News of her sinking reached Germany from the USA where it was published in the newspapers and caused a great sensation. The Germans were furious.

A number of decorations were awarded to the crew of *Baralong* for this operation, also the sum of £1000. This success was very welcome, following as it did a terrible toll of shipping losses; it also convinced the British authorities of the value of 'Q' ships. It was decided that several more steamers should be fitted out as decoy ships to help counter the submarine menace.

Two decoy tramp steamers were accordingly prepared and assigned to Queenstown. These were *Zylpha* (2,917 tons) and *Lodorer* (3,207 tons). The former was sunk on 15 June, after doing excellent service, and the latter, under the aliases of *Farnborough* and *Q5*, and commanded by Commander Gordon Campbell, RN, became the most famous of all the decoy ships and achieved imperishable renown, as did her gallant commander.

After a number of U-boats had been sunk by the mystery ships the Germans became very wary and were not easily deceived and it became quite customary for a 'Q' ship which had had some success to assume an alias. Before being appointed to 'Q' ships Gordon Campbell had been in command of the destroyer *Bittern*. It was on 21 October 1915 that he had commissioned the tramp steamer *Loderer* at Devonport as a 'Q' ship. But on passage thence to Queenstown her name was changed to *Farnborough* as a number of people came to know that *Loderer* was being equipped for special service. The ship was armed with five 12-pounders, two 6-pounders and one Maxim gun. Of the ship's complement, seven of the officers belonged to the Royal Navy and many of the ratings were either RN or RNVR.

Throughout the following winter months, enduring every type of foul weather, the ship's captain and crew, altered to look like tramp seamen, were trained to perfection for the task in hand. At the beginning of March 1916 the Germans renewed their submarine campaign with the greatest intensity. On the morning of 22 March *Farnborough*, coming from Queenstown, was cruising up the west coast of Ireland. Suddenly a submarine was sighted by one of the crew.

After a few minutes it dived and *Farnborough* continued steadily on her course as though she had seen nothing. Twenty minutes later the U-boat fired a torpedo which passed close across the bows of the ship. *Farnborough* went on her way without apparently having seen it. A few minutes later the submarine surfaced about 1000 yards astern and, having positioned herself to do so, fired a shell across the ship's bows.

Farnborough at once stopped her engines, blew off steam and ordered the 'panic party', under Engineer Sub-Lieutenant J. S. Smith, RNR, and consisting of stokers and spare men, to abandon ship. The submarine then came closer, seeing no human movement on the ship, where everyone was lying concealed. It became apparent that the submarine intended to sink the ship, but her first shell fell fifty yards short. This was the moment of fate and *Farnborough*'s one and only chance. Commander Gordon Campbell had only seconds in which to make his decision. It was a question of which vessel scored the first hit. Without hesitation Campbell ordered the White Ensign to be hoisted and fire to be opened. The submarine was swept by a hail of shells and intensive Maxim and rifle fire.

Despite the rather poor light the 'Q' ship's fire was extremely accurate – as it had to be. The submarine was badly holed and began to submerge. Campbell steamed full speed towards the U-boat and dropped a depth charge. This forced the submarine to the surface in an almost perpendicular position. Now, going for the kill, *Farnborough* put five shells into the base of the conning-tower at point-blank range, and the U-boat sank like a stone. Two more depth charges completed her end and brought to the surface a large quantity of oil and debris which covered the sea for some distance around. The U-boat was one of the latest German submarines, armed with one 4.1-inch gun, one 22-pounder, a machine-gun and eleven torpedoes. She had a speed of seventeen knots and a cruising radius of 11,000 miles.

The saying 'It is strange that a man should miss when his life depends on his aim', was certainly true of this engagement. The submarine had first strike – and missed. Had it been on target the result of the encounter would have been entirely reversed. The German gun-layer was careless, thinking he was dealing with just another unarmed merchantman which could be sunk just as well with the second shot as with the first. The very highly trained crew of the 'Q' ship knew that their first salvo would be their last if it wasn't quick and dead on target. Campbell was awarded a DSO. In less than a month *Farnborough* engaged another submarine which got away under a smoke screen, damaged but not destroyed.

On 17 February 1917 Commander Campbell, still in command of *Farnborough*, which was now officially named *Q5,* sank another submarine which won for him the Victoria Cross. The scene of this action was once more off the south-west Irish coast. The Germans had started their unrestricted submarine campaign rather earlier than usual. Their orders were to attack every Allied merchant ship they met, in waters as near the English coast as possible; any steamers were to be treated as hostile warships and sunk without notice. Their object was to cut Britain off from overseas supplies. As a precaution against possible decoy ships the orders were that when a ship had been abandoned she was to be sunk at once by gun-fire from an aft position so that ships' guns could not be brought to bear on the submarine. The 'Q' ships therefore had to use intensified deception – and even greater courage and skill – to fool the U-boats, even to the extent of deliberately taking a torpedo.

At 9.45 am on this fateful day *Farnborough* was struck by a torpedo which caused a terrific explosion and made a huge hole in the ship's side. An engineer sub-lieutenant was wounded. The 'Action' signal was given and the ship was abandoned by all spare members of the crew, who embarked in two lifeboats and one dinghy and were lowering a fourth. The ship was obviously sinking. The submarine was the *U 83,* one of Germany's newest, commanded by Lieutenant-Commander Bruno Hoppe.

Campbell saw the submarine's periscope appearing on the starboard side of the ship, only 200 yards away. Still submerged the *U 83* began making a thorough scrutiny of the 'Q' ship. The temptation for *Farnborough* to open fire was almost unbearable, and there might never be another chance. The submarine passed round the ship, but saw no sign of life. Then, not wanting to waste another precious torpedo, she surfaced about 300 yards away on the port bow. Still *Farnborough* held her fire. *U 83* made a closer scrutiny from the surface, but with much less caution now.

Campbell waited until all his guns could bear and then the White Ensign was hoisted and at point-blank range he delivered the knock-out blow. The first shot, from one of *Farnborough*'s 6-pounders, hit the U-boat's conning-tower and beheaded the German commander. The submarine's hull was shattered. Surprise was complete and *U 83* never recovered. Finally she turned over and sank just as several of her crew appeared from the conning-tower and jumped into the sea. Campbell ceased fire at once to go to their assistance and picked up one officer and one man alive.

The sea was thick with oil, blood and wreckage. All the time the fight was on the Chief Engineer and his staff remained in the flooded engine room and kept the dynamos and machinery going until driven out by the inrushing water. *Farnborough* was sinking by the stern. Captain Campbell wirelessed for help and HM Sloop *Buttercup* arrived and took her in tow. The gallant 'Q' ship had survived a number of actions through the skill and courage of her captain and crew and by reason of the fact that her holds were packed with timber which kept her afloat when most other ships would have sunk. Later she was repaired, refloated and reconditioned and went back to the Merchant Service as a cargo carrier. Her days as a 'Q' ship were over.

Other 'Q' ships commanded by Captain Campbell performed gallant and distinguished service in the vital battle with the U-boats in the Atlantic. The first was on 7 June 1917 in HMS *Pargust,* when two VCs were awarded to the ship and, by selection of the ship's company, given to Lieutenant R. N. Stuart, DSO, RNR, and Seaman W. Williams, RNR. The second was on 8 August 1917 in HMS *Dunraven* when, once again, two VCs were awarded to the ship and those chosen to receive the Cross were Lieutenant C. G. Bonner, DSC, RN, and Petty Officer E. Pitcher, RNR. Although in this latter case the submarine escaped complete destruction, this was Captain Campbell's greatest action, and probably the greatest of all 'Q' ship actions, for which he could well have been awarded a bar to his VC. He did marvels to save his ship which was twice torpedoed. In his report to the Admiralty Captain Campbell wrote:

'We desired nothing better, not only to destroy the enemy and save the ship, but also to show ourselves worthy of the VCs which were presented to the ship.'

Lieutenant Bonner's VC was announced in the Court Circular issued from York Cottage, Sandringham on Sunday, 8 October 1917, before the award was announced in the *London Gazette,* and it was on this day that he received the Cross. This may well have been the only occasion when a man received the vc from the Sovereign's hand on a Sunday.

No account of this grim struggle which these brave tramp steamers waged against the U-boats would be complete without describing the action which won a posthumous vc for Skipper Thomas Crisp, RNR, who was commanding a 'special ship', known as an 'armed smack', called *Nelson*. He was aged forty-two at the time.

On the afternoon of 15 August 1917, when the Skipper was below packing fish, a German submarine was spotted on the horizon, which almost immediately opened fire. *Nelson* was cleared for action just as a shell hit the ship below the water line. The gun-layer of *Nelson*'s gun replied as best he could against the hail of fire which engulfed them. The Skipper cooly directed operations. Then a shell passed clean through the ship and mortally wounded him. Before he died he dictated a wireless message: '*Nelson* being attacked by submarine. Skipper killed. Send assistance at once.' He then gave the order to abandon ship, which was rapidly sinking, and, with a smile on his face, he went down with his ship. Truly the Skipper of *Nelson* did not need the signal of the famous admiral: 'England expects each man this day to do his duty.'

17

Five Padre vcs

Throughout British history most great generals have realized the importance of religion to the morale of men in battle. Marlborough, Sir John Moore, Wellington, Lord Roberts, and more recently, Haig, Wavell, Montgomery, Alexander and Slim, all put emphasis and importance on the spiritual well-being of their armies and their own relationships with their chaplains. From every battle front in both World Wars of 1914-18 and 1939-45 there have been inspiring stories about chaplains. Many of them made a point of being in the danger areas with the troops but only five padres won the Victoria Cross. Padres, of course, were knights without armour.

The first was the Reverend J. W. Adams of the Bengal Ecclesiastical Department at Killa Kazi in the Afghan War on 11 December 1879. John William Adams was born at Cork in 1839 and had become chaplain of the Bengal Establishment at Calcutta in October 1866. In November 1878 he was summoned to join the Kurram Field Force and then accompanied the Kabul Field Force under Sir Donald Stewart and Sir Frederick Roberts. He took part in the historic Kabul to Kandahar march under the latter.

On 11 December 1879 Padre Adams risked his life at Killa Kazi when he went to the rescue of some men of the 9th Lancers who had fallen into a deep nullah and were struggling underneath their horses whilst under heavy fire from the Afghans. For this gallant act Sir Frederick Roberts (later Field-Marshal Lord Roberts) recommended him for the Victoria Cross, but this was turned down on the grounds that the vc was for the Army and Navy only. In the *London Gazette* of 24 August

1881 it was announced that : 'The Queen had been pleased by Royal Warrant to direct that the Victoria Cross should be conferred on members of the Indian Ecclesiastical Establishment who might be qualified' and that accordingly she had conferred this high distinction on the Reverend J. W. Adams. Roberts was indeed a power in the land and a great favourite with the queen.

The Reverend Edward Noel Mellish was thirty-six years old when he won his VC at St Eloi, France on 27/29 March 1916. He had previously served in the South African War as a trooper in Baden-Powell's Police.

Padre Mellish, as he was usually called, was attached to the Royal Fusiliers during the three days' hectic fighting round St Eloi, in which heavy casualties were suffered. He repeatedly went backwards and forwards under heavy shell and machine-gun fire between our original trenches and those captured from the Germans in order to tend and rescue the wounded. He brought in ten badly wounded men on the first day from ground swept by machine-gun fire, three of whom were hit again and killed while he was dressing their wounds. The battalion to which he was attached was relieved on the second day, but Padre Mellish went back and brought in twelve more of their wounded. On the night of the third day he took charge of a party of volunteers and once more returned to the trenches to rescue a number of the wounded who were still lying out in no-man's-land. This splendid work on his part was quite outside the scope of his ordinary duties.

The Reverend William Addison won his VC for conspicuous bravery at Sannaiyat, Mesopotamia, on 9 April 1916. He carried a wounded man to the cover of a trench and assisted several others to the same cover, after binding up their wounds under heavy rifle and machine-gun fire. In addition to these unaided efforts, by his splendid example and complete disregard for personal danger, he encouraged the stretcher-bearers to go forward as well to bring in more of the wounded men lying out in the open. He was also awarded the Russian Order of St George.

The Reverend Theodore Bayley Hardy, DSO, MC, of the Army Chaplains' Department (attached 8th Battalion Lincolnshire Regiment) won his VC near Bucquoy, east of Gommecourt, in France, for his gallantry during the period 25/27 April 1918.

Theodore Hardy was really a disciple of another very famous Army chaplain, Geoffrey Studdert-Kennedy, more commonly known as 'Woodbine Willie'. So great a man as William Temple, later Archbishop of Canterbury, thought that Studdert-Kennedy, in his capacity to move men's hearts, was the finest priest he had ever known – and as a mover of men's hearts William Temple himself was very hard to beat.

In appearance Studdert-Kennedy was insignificant : small, with bat-ears, large brown eyes and generally untidily dressed. He could swear like a trooper – and often did – and was anathema to many orthodox general officers in the Army. For much of his life he was afflicted with asthma and he eventually worked himself into an early grave. His courage shone like a flame and he would never give in. He was awarded the MC for gallantry at Messines in 1917. He was essentially a front-line padre and much as he often hated it, he felt he had to go where his men went. Before a trench raid he would hold a Service for the men who were to undertake it, gathered round him in their tin hats with blackened faces. He did not have to suggest a Service, the men did, and that strengthened the bonds between them enormously.

When Theodore Hardy, who became the most decorated of all Army chaplains, first came out to France he asked Studdert-Kennedy to advise him as to the best way of working. The latter replied :

'Live with the men, go everywhere they go. Make up your mind you will share their risks, and more, if you can do any good. The front line is the key to the whole business. Work in the very front and they will listen to you ; but if you stay behind you are wasting your time. Men will forgive you anything but lack of courage and devotion.'

Theodore Hardy was determined to follow Studdert-Kennedy's advice. After many other acts of gallantry which won for him the DSO and the MC, he won his VC 'For most conspicuous bravery on many occasions. Although over fifty years of age he has by his fearless devotion to the men of his battalion and quiet unobtrusive manner, won the respect and admiration of the whole division. His marvellous energy and endurance would be remarkable in a very much younger man.'

Hardy had followed a patrol 400 yards beyond the front line to help bring in a wounded officer and remained with him until he could get some stretcher-bearers to bring him in. Then, when an enemy shell exploded in one of the British posts and several men were buried, he went forward under heavy fire and managed to dig two of them out alive. A third time he went out to a most exposed position within a few yards of a German pill-box and helped a sergeant bring in a badly wounded man.

Wherever he could be of help this very gallant chaplain was seen, moving quietly amongst the men and tending the wounded, absolutely regardless of his personal safety. Everyone knew that his end was inevitable and he was killed in action on 18 October 1918, only two months after his award of the vc had been gazetted.

The Commanding Officer of the 8th Lincolns wrote to a member of Hardy's family :

He appealed to us all, both officers and men, by his absolute fearlessness, physical and moral, and by his simple sincerity and lack of cant and humbug. We loved him for his self-effacing devotion to duty. His gallantry in action won him distinction which will make his name famous in history, and yet his retiring nature made it almost a penance for him to wear those ribbons which most of us would give our right arm for. What his loss has meant to us is more than I can ever express.

The fifth and last Padre vc was won by the Reverend John Weir Foote, Canadian Army Chaplain at Dieppe on 19 August 1942, which incident has been described in an earlier chapter.

18

The Model Battle of Hamel.

The action which took place at Hamel, north-west of Villiers-Bretonneux, on 4 July 1918 by troops of General Rawlinson's 4th Army marked not only a turning point in tank warfare but a turning point in the war itself, which certainly accelerated our final victory.

The credit for the success of this action at Hamel must be given primarily to two men, Colonel Fuller and General Rawlinson. Fuller, who was Chief of Staff to the Tank Corps at the time, was one of the pioneers of tank warfare and one of the most brilliant brains in the British Army. He had been trying to impress upon all the Allied Commanders the merits of the new Mark v tank which was being produced in England in large numbers by the beginning of 1918 and he found Winston Churchill a great ally in his endeavours.

Rawlinson was always seeking to solve the problem of the breaking of the trench barrier. A long drawn-out preliminary bombardment had seemed the only answer in all the great battles on the Western Front. This procedure, however, destroyed all chance of surprise, churned up the ground, cut all the communications and resulted in long and bloody encounters in which the results were often not commensurate with the casualties suffered.

At Hamel as few infantry as possible and as many tanks as possible were employed. No preliminary bombardment preceded the attack and the covering artillery barrage opened at zero hour, 3.10 am, which was also the time set for the infantry to advance. The tanks and infantry advanced together behind the barrage. By 5 am the attack was over. The Germans put up a good fight but they were surprised and then overwhelmed, first by the great wall of artillery fire which suddenly descended upon them and then by the immediate arrival of the tanks. The British artillery did brilliantly in the counter-battery work so that the attackers were not troubled by German artillery fire. The usual difficulty of getting ammunition and supplies forward was solved by parachute drops from aircraft and by the supply tanks which delivered barbed wire, screw pickets, corrugated iron, hand grenades, ammunition and drinking water (plus a good dollop of Scotch whisky and rum). Thus, instead of the infantry having to advance laden like beasts of burden, as they had done at the Somme, they were able to go into the attack in light fighting order.

The total Australian losses, killed and wounded, were only 672; of the sixty tanks, fifty-eight reached their objectives and fifty-five returned to their rallying points. Of the tank personnel no single officer or man was killed and only thirteen other ranks wounded.

The brilliance of the tanks' performance must not be allowed to obscure the gallantry of the small numbers of Australian infantry who had still to consolidate the ground the tanks had gained and resist the inevitable German counter-attack. Lance-Corporal Axford's platoon had reached the enemy defences when a machine-gun on the flank came into action and inflicted a number of casualties, including the company commander. Lance-Corporal Axford attacked the machine-gun crew with bomb and bayonet, killed ten of the enemy and took six prisoners. His initiative and gallantry prevented many casualties and greatly contributed to the success of his company in gaining its objective.

Driver Henry Dalziel won his vc for most conspicuous bravery and devotion to duty when in action with a Lewis gun section. His company met with determined resistance from a strongpoint which was heavily garrisoned and manned by numerous machine-guns. These caused a number of casualties and held up the advance. He had brought his Lewis gun into action effectively in one direction when an enemy gun opened fire from another. Driver Dalziel attacked it single-handed and killed or captured the entire gun crew, which allowed the advance to continue. He was severely wounded but carried on to the capture of the final objective. He twice went over open ground under heavy fire to secure ammunition and continued to serve his gun until again severely wounded in the head. His magnificent courage was an inspiring example to his comrades.

This action at Hamel was a great morale-raiser. General Fuller wrote later :

'Though we did not realize it at the time, on 3 July 1918 we were no more than a poor street singer but on the fourth that singer was standing on the stage of a great opera house deafened by applause.'

19

Between the Two World Wars.

As I was personally involved in all of these incidents and with the VCs concerned I have expanded on some of the details. The first inter-war VC was awarded to Captain H. J. Andrews, Indian Medical Service, posthumously, for his bravery when the Mahsuds attacked a convoy on 22 October 1919 in Waziristan.

Early in May 1919 the Third Afghan War started and the 43rd Infantry Brigade, of which I was brigade-major, was ordered to move up to the frontier. The Afghans gave us little trouble but the rising of the formidable frontier tribesmen, the Wazirs and the Mahsuds, which followed, was far more menacing and gave rise to the toughest campaign the British had ever experienced on the north-west frontier of India.

All that summer in blistering heat before the Waziristan campaign proper began the 43rd Brigade, stationed at Idak in the Tochi valley, was guarding the long lines of communication which were always so vulnerable to the tribesmen's attack. On 22 October 1919 an animal convoy, seven miles long, was moving up the line from Bannu, protected by road piquets and by a certain number of infantry soldiers marching with the column.

On the evening of the twenty-first a raiding party of about a hundred Mahsuds had come over the mountains into the Tochi valley and hidden themselves in the rocks on one side of the road, quite close to the small fortified post of Khajuri, where the road debouched from the Shinki Pass. With amazing forbearance they had allowed the brigade commander, Brigadier-General Gwyn-Thomas, to pass through when he motored right under their noses on his way from Bannu back to brigade headquarters at Idak. How their mouths must have watered at the sight of his rotund figure in a red hat ; but they lay doggo until next day and the head of the convoy had got well past Khajuri post. Then they suddenly opened fire and the road became a shambles of dead and wounded men and animals. The Mahsuds planned to keep the road covered and the convoy halted, until darkness set in when they could loot the convoy at their leisure.

The officer commanding the small garrison of Khajuri, though he was closely confined by the fire of the Mahsuds to his post, managed to get through on the civil telephone to brigade headquarters at Idak and reported the situation. If anything possible could be done to rescue this large and valuable convoy it had to be done with speed.

General Gwyn-Thomas asked me to set off immediately with the only two rather antiquated armoured cars available and 300 men of the 9th Jats under command of Major McCalmont in Ford vans. The officer commanding Khajuri post was advised and asked to co-operate with me in any way he could. We arrived on the scene in about two hours with not many hours of daylight left.

I halted the column at a vantage point, where we debussed, and had a short conference with Major McCalmont, a grand fighting soldier whom I knew well, and a young officer in charge of the armoured cars. The tribesmen hated to have enemy troops on the high hills above them, so that I sent McCalmont on a roundabout route to do just that and so to make his presence seen and felt as quickly as possible. My greatest worry was for the wounded lying about in heaps around the scene of action. No one who has ever seen the ghastly result of leaving a man in the hands of the tribesmen would ever willingly do so again. Rudyard Kipling knew the form when he wrote :

> When you're wounded and left on Afghanistan's plains
> And the women come out to cut up what remains
> Just roll to your rifle and blow out your brains
> And go to your Gawd like a soldier.

I did not know that in Khajuri post there was a medical officer of great courage, with a medical section, who by his utter disregard of his own safety and with the help of the Ford vans, would play a great part in taking that worry off my shoulders – at the cost of his own life.

First we had to deal with the Mahsuds who seemed to hold all the cards. As soon as McCalmont and his men were well on their way I rammed the two armoured cars straight down the road into the middle of the carnage created by the Mahsuds, to take them on at point blank range. For several minutes it was touch and go, the Mahsuds resisting strongly with their modern rifles and smokeless powder, invisible among the rocks. The trouble was that our old armoured cars were bullet proof only in parts and one or two of the crews were getting hit through the armour. But the blistering fire of the machine-guns at a hundred yards range and the sight of McCalmont's men climbing up on the high hills was too much for the marauders. They vacated their position, leaving several dead men behind, and retired to a concealed position further back, from which they could still bring fire to bear on the road.

Despite this, Captain Andrews of the Indian Medical Service, who was quite an elderly man, at once emerged from Khajuri post with some medical orderlies, and reported to me. He then set up an aid post and took complete charge of the rescue, treatment and evacuation of the wounded. He set a magnificent example, having no thought for his own safety and continued his work with the wounded in spite of a heavy fire from the Mahsuds. I had put as many vans at his disposal as he required and, having loaded them with wounded, he was killed as he was stepping into the last van.

With McCalmont's Jats bringing fire to bear on the Mahsuds from the heights above they beat a hasty retreat and we were able to get the convoy safely through and encamped before darkness set in. Captain Andrews was awarded a posthumous Victoria Cross and McCalmont and I got the MC.

Captain Andrews had been an officer in the Salvation Army for over thirty years and it was to him that the Salvation Army owed the commencement of their work in India.

The next Victoria Cross was awarded to Lieutenant William David Kenny of the 4/39th Garhwal Rifles at Kot Kai in Waziristan on 2 January 1920. It was two months later and we were in the throes of the Mahsud campaign. In 1919, as part of the Tochi Column, we had advanced on the Wazir capital and forced them to accept our terms. It was decided that the same two infantry brigades, under command of that splendid general, Andrew Skeen, should form the Derajat Column against the Mahsuds. They were generally acknowledged to be the toughest fighters of all the Indian tribesmen and in my experience amongst the finest soldiers in the world. Fighting in their own craggy mountains, and containing many men who had served in the Indian Army, and more still who had deserted from the frontier militias, they were at the top of their form ; whereas the British troops, in the throes of demobilization after the First World War, were mostly inexperienced in mountain warfare.

From the start the column experienced the fiercest opposition from the Mahsuds and had suffered several costly and humiliating reverses. The position was so serious that General Skeen flew to Delhi and was promised an immediate reinforcement of four battalions of Gurkhas.

General Skeen had been forced to accept the procedure of erecting permanent piquets to protect his lines of communication and in some cases it had taken a whole brigade operation to establish one permanent piquet.

On 2 January 1920 the 4/39th Garhwalis, as fine a battalion as I have ever seen, was ordered to construct a permanent piquet about 2,500 yards from our brigade perimeter camp. The morale of the Mahsuds was at this time sky high as a result of their successes. The 4/39th started at first light so as to take advantage of every hour of daylight, which were never enough for an operation of this nature. The Mahsuds did not lie out on the cold hillside all night in this bitter winter weather – they did not have the warm clothing for it – and they let the Garhwalis' advance go unopposed. We had learnt to our cost that this did not mean that there would not be some very fierce fighting later on, and it was always in following up a withdrawal that the Mahsuds were most dangerous. The exact site of the piquet had been chosen by General Skeen himself, and no one had a better eye for ground than he.

Lieutenant-Colonel Lane, the first-class commanding officer of the Garhwalis, disposed his battalion to protect the building of the piquet and also with a view to the withdrawal later on in the afternoon. The Sappers and Pioneers, together with the garrison of the piquet, a hundred men from another Indian battalion, at once began building the piquet with stone sangars. Then it would have to be wired, stocked with ten days' rations and water and left out in the blue, with its garrison of 100 men, to the tender mercies of the Mahsuds.

My job as brigade-major, as representative of General Gwyn-Thomas, was to be out on the hillside with the co about 12.30. The time of the withdrawal was fixed at 3 pm to enable the troops to be back inside the perimeter well before darkness set in. There were two all-important decisions to be made. First and foremost, was the building of the piquet sufficiently far advanced for it to be left out, or should the project be postponed for another day. In which case all the ten days' supplies, the sandbags and the wire and the water would have to be carted back to camp well before the withdrawal started. I had seen the ghastly results of being too optimistic over this where the Mahsuds had attacked an insufficiently fortified permanent piquet and annihilated the garrison before we had returned to camp.

The second important point was to settle the plan for withdrawal – what covering fire could be given with the mountain guns and would the support of another battalion be required? Both these problems depended in this case on Lieutenant William David Kenny, who was commanding a company holding the key defence position on a knife-edge ridge. Could he hold this position for another two hours to enable the piquet to be completed and, when the general withdrawal started at 3 pm, could he then hold it long enough to cover the withdrawal of the other companies and finally get away himself? The Mahsuds knew full well that this was the key position, as their attacks on Kenny's company were growing in intensity.

I accompanied Colonel Lane to see Kenny, tall, strong, red-haired, smiling, and as good a young subaltern as any battalion could wish to have. These young Indian Army British officers had great responsibilities as the full establishment of British officers in a battalion was only twelve, which meant that there were rarely more than eight present at any one time. Kenny's answer to all my questions was 'Yes', he could hold on for the required time. Whether he could ever get away himself was another matter which we did not of course discuss. I could only wish him good luck, but I feared that his broad smile and warm hand-shake might possibly be the last I should ever see of him. Before I left, however, Colonel Lane and I decided that, owing to the long-range sniping fire being brought to bear on the piquet builders, it could not be put in a proper state of defence before 3 pm and orders were at once given for the stores, the Pioneers and Sappers building the piquet and the garrison to be withdrawn to camp at once. Three days later we came out with a rather stronger force and finished the job, but not without a battle.

As soon as the withdrawal started the Mahsuds pressed upon Kenny from all sides but his company fought back fiercely in hand-to-hand fighting and never gave an inch, whilst the other companies got away. When his CO ordered him to withdraw he trickled three platoons away cleverly, remaining with the fourth platoon to give them cover. Then, after a final burst of fire, he got them away as well, but on the way down the hill he saw one of the other platoons having difficulty in withdrawing some wounded men. Obeying the frontier code of never leaving a wounded man to the tender mercies of the tribesmen he at once ordered the platoon he was with to turn about, fix bayonets and charge the rapidly pursuing Mahsuds. It was, of course, certain death and Kenny and all his party were killed – but the wounded men were carried to safety.

Kenny was awarded a very well-deserved posthumous VC. The 4/39th had displayed the greatest gallantry and fighting skill and the Mahsuds ever afterwards treated them with deepest respect.

The third inter-war VC went to Captain George Stuart Henderson, DSO, MC, of the 2nd Manchester Regiment in the Arab Insurrection in Mesopotamia on 24 July 1920.

George Henderson and I were almost exact contemporaries, he being born two months after me, in December 1893. He was at Sandhurst a year after me (in 1912) and also, like me, wanted Indian Army, but only passed out 51st which was too low. However, he achieved his ambition to serve in India, being commissioned on 24 January 1914 into the Ist Manchester Regiment in Jullundur.

On 29 August 1914 we embarked in the same troop-ship (I being in the 15th Sikhs) at Karachi for Marseilles in the Jullundur Brigade of the Lahore Division in the Indian Corps. For the next year we soldiered together in France, he winning the MC and I the VC. We were generally known as 'the babes' of the brigade. Squarely built and intrepid, with a pipe usually clenched in the corner of his mouth, he was a splendid type of regimental officer with marked powers of leadership.

When the Indian Corps left France in the latter part of 1915 our ways parted. George joined the 2nd Manchesters in Mesopotamia, where he won a DSO (having been recommended for a VC on that occasion). Curiously enough, we never served together again until the Arab Insurrection of 1920 in Mesopotamia, when he was a captain commanding a company of the 2nd Manchesters and I was Brigade Major 74th Infantry Brigade. I was most distressed to hear of his death in an ambush by a large force of Arabs near Hillah on 24 June 1920, but rejoiced that he had been awarded a posthumous VC.

His citation read as follows :

On the evening of 24 July Captain Henderson's company was ordered to retire. After proceeding about 500 yards a large party of Arabs suddenly opened fire from the flank, causing the company to split up and waver. Regardless of all danger Captain Henderson at once reorganized the company, led them gallantly to the attack and drove off the enemy. On two further occasions this officer led his men to charge the Arabs with the bayonet and forced them to retire. At one time, when the situation was extremely critical and the troops and transport were getting out of hand, Captain Henderson, by sheer pluck and coolness, steadied his command, prevented the company from being cut up and saved the situation.

During the second charge he fell wounded but refused to leave his command, and just as the company was reaching the trench they were making for he was again wounded. Realizing he could do no more he asked one of the NCOs to hold him up on the embankment, saying : 'I'm done now, don't let them beat you.' He died fighting.

George Henderson's sister, Jess, aged twenty-four, went to Buckingham Palace on 8 March 1921 to receive her brother's cross from King George V. The King had written on 29 November 1920 to George's father :

'It is a matter of sincere regret to me that the death of Captain George Stuart Henderson, DSO, MC, 2nd Battalion Manchester Regiment, deprived me of the pride of personally conferring upon him the Victoria Cross, the greatest of all rewards for valour and devotion to duty.'

The 2nd Manchesters' casualties in this action were 179 killed, sixty wounded and seventy-eight taken prisoner.

Sepoy Ishar Singh was with the 28th Punjabis on convoy protection duty when, near Haidari Kach, Waziristan, on 10 April 1921, the convoy was attacked by a large party of tribesmen. Ishar Singh was number one of a Lewis gun section. Early in the action he received a very severe gunshot wound in the chest and fell beside his Lewis gun. The tribesmen came to close quarters and in the hand-to-hand fighting which ensued the British officer, one Indian officer and all the non-commissioned officers of his company were either killed or wounded and his Lewis gun was seized by the enemy.

Calling upon two other men Ishar Singh got up, recovered his Lewis gun and, although bleeding profusely, got the gun into action. When his jemadar arrived he ordered Ishar Singh to go back to the aid post and have his wound dressed. Ishar Singh, however, insisted on carrying water to the wounded and made a number of journeys to the river and back for this purpose, always under fire. On one occasion he took the rifle of a wounded man and engaged the enemy. On another occasion he sheltered the medical officer from enemy fire with his own body whilst the latter was attending to a badly wounded man. It was over three hours before he finally became so weak from loss of blood that he allowed himself to become evacuated. His conduct was an inspiration to all who saw him.

Ishar Singh was decorated with the Victoria Cross by the Prince of Wales at a review of the Rawalpindi Division held on the parade ground at Rawalpindi on 10 March 1922.

In 1929 Ishar Singh, now a subadar, attended the vc reunion in London. He was placed in my charge and I took him back to India with me on the P and O *Viceroy of India* (sunk in the Second World War) afterwards. On Monday, 11 November 1929 the Remembrance Service took place at the Cenotaph when, for the first and only time, the vcs marched on to the parade as a body. Nearly 300 vcs assembled in Wellington Barracks, each wearing a Flanders poppy with his medals. When the order to fall in was given I inserted myself and Ishar Singh, conspicuous in his Sikh *pagri* (turban) in the very last row of fours. However, in manoeuvring us out of the barracks, the officer in charge of the parade about-turned us and Ishar Singh and I thus marched on to this historic parade in the front row of fours. The Daily Sketch wrote :

Of all the crowds we have seen assemble in Whitehall on successive Armistice days this was the most silent. There was, however, one long spontaneous cheer from the crowd before the service when the VCs came marching on.

The VCs were ranked like a deep wall across the width of the roadway. The variety of civilian costume, including one or two silk hats, would not alone have marked them out from the other ex-Servicemen but for the Crosses they all wore and the great wreath in the same symbol placed in front of them to be laid presently on the Cenotaph. Near the centre of them a small girl in school dress, with a deep crepe band on her arm, and bearing a small wreath, stood in this front row of Britain's bravest. The girl was the daughter of a VC and was wearing her father's medal. The veteran VC who accompanied her was her maternal grandfather. She placed the wreath immediately after the big VC wreath was laid.

The Prime Minister, Ramsay Macdonald, accompanied by the Speaker of the House of Commons, Stanley Baldwin, and Lloyd George, stood in front of the Home Office. Just before 11 am the Prince of Wales (the King was not well enough to attend) took his place wearing the uniform of the Welsh Guards. As Big Ben struck the first note of the Armistice hour a gun boomed and the two-minute silence began.

Ishar Singh and I remained friends until his death. His VC was sold at an auction in London on 4 July 1970 for the then record price of £2000. In 1976 a VC was sold for over £7000. When King George V gave me my VC he gave me a plain cardboard box to go with it so that, in his own words, 'the intrinsic value of the Cross and the box should not be more than one penny'. The Cross was, of course, made from a Russian cannon captured at Sebastopol in the Crimean War.

The last of the inter-war VCs was awarded posthumously to Captain Godfrey Meynell, MC, 5th Battalion Queen Victoria's Own Corps of Guides, 12th FFR, Indian Army, on 29 September 1935 in the Mohmand Campaign on the north-west frontier of India.

It was in this campaign that Field-Marshal Sir Claude Auchinleck, as a brigadier (acting major-general) first made his name as a leader of troops in action. He was commander of the Peshawar Brigade and as the senior brigadier was appointed MOHFORCE commander. Brigadier Alexander (later Field-Marshal) was commanding the Nowshera Brigade and I was a lieutenant-colonel commanding the 45th Sikhs in the Rawalpindi Brigade, commanded by Brigadier Cyril Noyes.

There was a good deal of sharp fighting and a lot of unspectacular but essential piquetting and convoying before the tribal forces were defeated. Towards the end of the operations, when it was believed that the tribesmen were dispersing and intending to sue for peace, a minor disaster occurred, which did not involve Auchinleck's Peshawar Brigade. It was in an isolated attack following a night advance, that the famous Guides Battalion was ambushed by a powerful and well-concealed body of tribesmen, and Captain Godfrey Meynell, the adjutant of the battalion, won his posthumous Victoria Cross.

Such operations demanded complete secrecy and on this occasion the Mohmands had somehow got wind of the move and were out on the hillside in large numbers. When the battalion commander received no report from his forward company, who should have arrived at the objective, Captain Meynell went forward to ascertain the situation. He found the company on the objective but involved in a tough struggle with a body of tribesmen vastly superior in numbers. Captain Meynell gathered together, and took command of, about thirty men and two Lewis guns and endeavoured to restore the situation. The enemy were closing in on the position from three sides. Both the Lewis guns were put out of action and a fierce hand-to-hand struggle took place.

Captain Meynell showed inspiring leadership and was intrumental in preventing the enemy from exploiting their success. He was mortally wounded and the battalion suffered some heavy casualties, totalling two British officers and two Indian officers killed, four British officers and two Indian officers wounded, one British other rank and thirty Indian other ranks killed and one British and forty-seven Indian other ranks wounded. These were very heavy casualties indeed for an operation of this nature, but although this success gave the Mohmands' morale a boost it was not sufficient to prevent them suing for peace.

20

The Sinking of HMS *Glowworm.*

The first major offensive move in the Second World War directly affecting the British was made by the Germans in April 1940, when they invaded Denmark and Norway by sea and air. In less than twelve hours the Germans were masters of Oslo and of all the main ports and airfields in Norway. Meanwhile in London, Winston Churchill, First Lord of the Admiralty, had persuaded Prime Minister Chamberlain, whom he was soon to succeed, to permit mining the Leads. The object of this was to stop the traffic of Swedish iron ore to Germany by the Narvik to the Skagerak route through Norwegian territorial waters. While the British Home Fleet remained at Scapa Flow, eight destroyers were despatched to lay a minefield in Vestfjorden and a mine-layer, escorted by four destroyers, was to lay another minefield between Trondheim and Bergen and two more destroyers were to mark a dummy field. Later the battle-cruiser *Renown*, with a screen of four destroyers – *Greyhound*, *Glowworm*, *Hyperion* and *Hero* – was sent to reinforce the Vestfjorden force.

HMS *Glowworm* was a destroyer of 1348 tons, carrying four 4.7 guns and torpedoes. The ship's complement was 140, including the commander, Gerard Broadmead Roope, Lieutenant Boothby and the torpedo control officer, Lieutenant R.A. Ramsay. Commander Roope was aged thirty-five. He had been in the Navy for twenty-two years and had been in command of *Glowworm* since July 1938. He was an utterly dedicated 'destroyer man', devoted to his ship and his crew, as they were to him, and brought up in the strictest traditions of the Royal Navy. Lieutenant Robert Ramsay was twenty-two.

On 7th April British aircraft found and bombed, without effect, German warships steaming north in company. Group 1 of this force comprised the battle cruisers *Gneisenau* and *Scharnhorst,* escorting ten destroyers carrying troops to Narvik. Group 2 was the cruiser *Hipper* and four destroyers carrying troops bound for Trondheim.

On the night of 7 April a gale arose which swept the Norwegian sea and made visibility difficult. It also threw the German destroyer groups into disorder. Just before dawn on the eighth a wave swept an able seaman overboard from *Glowworm*'s quarter-deck and Roope decided he must stop and search for him. The commander continued the search for two hours until all hope of finding him had been abandoned.

Renown and her escorting destroyers were observing radio silence and by this time Roope had lost touch with the other ships. As the weather worsened he had to reduce speed to less than ten knots. *Glowworm*'s gyro-compass failed and she had to steer by magnetic compass.

Suddenly, at 7.10 am, a destroyer, the *Hans Lüdemann,* appeared out of the haze on the port beam. *Glowworm* immediately challenged this ship and she replied that she was Swedish – and then at once opened fire. *Glowworm* replied with her 4.7s and a few moments later another destroyer appeared, the *Bernd Von Arnim. Glowworm* engaged them both and scored a hit on one of them, but lost two men overboard and had several more injured from her violent manoeuvring in the heavy seas. The enemy ships broke off action, the *Bernd Von Arnim* plunging and rolling so badly that her superstructure was badly damaged and she all but capsized. Although Commander Roope realized that they might be trying to lead him on to something more powerful, he decided to shadow them.

On the last morning of his life – and that of his ship – Roope sent out two signals: the first at 7.59, 'Unknown destroyer sighted – am engaging'; the second at 8.55, stating the arrival of the heavy German cruiser *Hipper,* 10,000 tons, carrying eight 8-inch, twelve 4.1-inch and twelve 37-mm guns. From that moment *Glowworm's* doom was sealed. She signalled that she was engaging enemy forces, and that was the last that was heard of her for five long years.

Four days later, on 11 April 1940, Winston Churchill, when reporting to the House of Commons that *Glowworm* had engaged enemy destroyers and then a heavy cruiser, said : 'The *Glowworm*'s light has been quenched.'

The rest of her story was known only after the war had ended and the survivors returned from the prisoner-of-war camp. Commander Roope's sole object had been to inflict as much damage as possible on the enemy cruiser before being sunk himself. *Hipper,* commanded by Captain Helmuth Heye, had answered *Bernd Von Arnim's* call for help and had come to remove this audacious British destroyer from the scene for good and all.

Hipper had at once opened fire beyond *Glowworm's* range with her 8-inch guns and battered her small opponent mercilessly. Almost at once *Glowworm's* bows were badly damaged, and a shell passed through her wheelhouse ; another burst in the transmitting station, killing most of the crew and all the staff of the wireless office. A third shell entered the ship under the after-torpedo tubes, crossed the ship and burst against the forward bulkhead of the captain's cabin. This shell also made a huge hole in the ship's side abreast of the engine room, while another shell wrecked the after superstructure.

As soon as *Glowworm* got within range she made smoke and Lieu-tenant Ramsay fired the torpedoes, which the Germans said afterwards had only narrowly missed the cruiser. *Glowworm* had by this time be-come a blazing inferno. One of her four guns was out of action. Her range-finder was hit. The upper yard of her mast had collapsed across the siren wires and her sirens were screeching amidst the blaze of battle and the smell of cordite and black smoke.

It was at this moment that Commander Roope decided, as a last desperate throw, to ram *Hipper.* He announced this decision to his number one, Lieutenant Boothby, in a calm, matter-of-fact voice. There was nothing to be said ; both men knew that *Glowworm* had reached the end of the road and all that mattered was to try to inflict the maximum damage on *Hipper.* If they could only put her out of action nothing would have been in vain.

Glowworm was now being raked by 8-inch and 4-inch shells and a hail of machine-gun fire. Roope ordered full speed ahead and in she went. Captain Heye tried desperately to take avoiding action, but it was too late, and *Glowworm's* bow crunched against the cruiser's side, tear-ing away a large part of her armoured belt and wrenching away her starboard torpedo tubes. As *Glowworm* drew away she fired one last shot and scored a hit on *Hipper.*

On *Glowworm's* bridge only Roope and Ramsay remained alive and the destroyer was listing dangerously with her torpedo tubes under water. Commander Roope gave the order to abandon ship. Great efforts were made to put life jackets on as many of the wounded and injured as possible. Chief Petty Officer Jack Townsend remembers his commander's last remark to him : 'I don't expect we'll play cricket together again'.

Just before 10 am *Glowworm* capsized and after floating bottom up for a few minutes she sank. The sea was dotted with bobbing heads as the men, mostly wounded and dying, tried to keep afloat. In the last hour of his life Roope's only thought was to support and encourage his wounded men, who were struggling to propel themselves towards *Hipper*, whose captain and crew could not have been more helpful and humane in extending to them all the aid they could. Only when he had done all he could for his men did Gerard Roope seek to save himself, and he had actually grasped the rope let down for him. But he was utterly exhausted; he had given everything, and he sank back into the sea and was drowned.

Lieutenant Ramsay had a life jacket but he was too spent to inflate it properly. Half-way to *Hipper* he lost consciousness, but he recovered, swam on and was eventually taken on board, where he was attended to by the German medical staff, together with the other survivors. He was devastated when he found that his gallant commander had not made it. Only thirty survivors were picked up by *Hipper*, the remaining 110 lost their lives in this heroic action. Two died in captivity and twenty-eight were repatriated at the end of the war, when, in addition to Commander Roope's posthumous VC, Lieutenant Ramsay was awarded the DSO and three ratings the Conspicuous Gallantry Medal.

All through the war in all the official records and in many books and articles, it had been stated that the first VC of the Second World War was that awarded to Captain Bernard Armitage Warburton-Lee, RN, who had been one of my pupils at the Camberley Staff College. He had won his VC, also posthumous, at Narvik on 10 April 1940, two days after Commander Roope. The full story of the latter's *Glowworm* experience was supplied after the war by the survivors and also by Captain Helmuth Heye, the German commander of *Hipper*, who was generous in his praise of Commander Roope. The latter's VC was then recognized as the first awarded in the Second World War.

Captain Warburton-Lee was a tall, handsome man, for whom I had the highest personal regard. He had assumed command of the destroyer HMS *Hardy* in August 1939. He had been warned on 2 April 1940, when in harbour at Scapa Flow, of 'Operation Wilfred' in which he was to take part in command of a flotilla of destroyers in Norwegian waters to cover a mine-laying operation. The flotilla left Scapa Flow at 6 pm on the second for the Shetlands, where they remained for two or three days, partly owing to the gales. They then set sail at 3 am on Saturday, 6 April, a little fleet of eight ships in all, with destroyers *Hardy*, *Hotspur*, *Hostile*, *Havock* and *Hunter*, together with the mine-layers. They had received orders to rendezvous with the battle cruiser *Renown* at 7.00 next morning. The weather was very rough and the destroyers were rolling heavily.

The weather improved as *Hardy* and three other destroyers, with the mine-layers, turned north inside the Lofoten Islands and steamed up Vestfjord. At dawn the mine-layers started laying their mines and the destroyers took up their protective positions. It had turned bitterly cold and the seas had become very rough. Warburton-Lee reported the mines successfuly laid and then proceeded to the rendezvous with *Renown*, which was not reached until 5 pm on the eighth owing to the bad weather and poor visibility. They had heard nothing of *Glowworm*'s action with *Hipper*.

On the night of 8/9 April the weather worsened and no one got any sleep. At 4 am on the ninth *Hardy* went to action stations. There was a lot of ice on the deck and heavy squalls of snow. An exchange of shots took place with unidentified German ships which drew off. *Renown* claimed two hits and had taken a shell through her bows without much damage, but *Renown*'s WT aerials had been shot away.

Then, at 11.30 came the dramatic order from the Admiralty to Warburton-Lee to take the five destroyers of his own flotilla – *Hardy*, *Hunter*, *Havock*, *Hotspur* and *Hostile* – and attack Narvik. Winston Churchill, then First Lord of the Admiralty, describes this operation in Volume I of his *History of the Second World War*. He makes it clear that the Admiralty was not prepared to risk the *Renown*, one of their only two battle cruisers, in such as enterprise, which must necessarily entail a large element of risk.

The weather continued to be quite appalling, with heavy seas, snow storms, much icing on the decks of the ships and very poor visibility. Winston Churchill writes :

Accordingly, Captain Warburton-Lee with the five destroyers entered Vestfjord. He had been told by Norwegian pilots at Tranoy that six German ships larger than his own and a U-boat had passed in to Narvik harbour and that the entrance was mined. He signalled this information to the Admiralty and added 'Intend attacking at dawn' (on 10 April).

The last Admiralty message passed to Captain Warburton-Lee at 1 am on the tenth was as follows :

'Norwegian coast defence troops may be in German hands, you alone can judge whether in these circumstances attack should be made. Shall support whatever decision you take.'

His reply was : 'Going into action'.

Warburton-Lee was very grateful to receive this signal and he took all possible steps to discover the strength of the opposition before committing all his ships to action.

Winston Churchill continues :

In the mist and snow-storms of 10 April the five British destroyers steamed up the fiord and at dawn stood off Narvik. Inside the harbour were five enemy destroyers. In the first attack *Hardy* torpedoed the ship bearing the pennant of the German Commodore, who was killed ; another destroyer was sunk by two torpedoes and the remaining three were so smothered by gun-fire that they could offer no effective resistance. Six German merchant ships were also destroyed. Only three of our five destroyers had hitherto attacked. *Hotspur* and *Hostile* had been kept in reserve. They now joined in a second attack and *Hotspur* sank two more merchantmen with torpedoes. Captain Warburton-Lee's ships were unscathed, the enemy's fire was apparently silenced and after an hour's fighting no ship had come out from any of the inlets against him.

Warburton-Lee consulted his Officers as to whether they should withdraw or go in again and finish the job. All were in favour of the latter course. What happened next was as much a surprise to the Admiralty as it was to Warburton-Lee and weighed the scales fatally against him.

Winston Churchill continues :

But now fortune turned. As he was coming back for a third attack Warburton-Lee sighted three fresh ships approaching from Herjangs Fiord.

They showed no sign of wishing to close the range and action began at 7000 yards. Suddenly out of the mist ahead appeared two more warships. They were not, as at first hoped, British reinforcements, but German destroyers which had been anchored in Ballengen Fiord. Soon the heavier guns of the German ships began to tell, the bridge of the *Hardy* was shattered, Warburton-Lee mortally stricken and all his officers and companions killed or wounded except Lieutenant Stanning, his secretary, who took the wheel. A shell then exploded in the engine room and under heavy fire the destroyer was beached. The last signal from the *Hardy*'s captain to his flotilla was : 'Continue to engage the enemy'.

Meanwhile *Hunter* had been sunk, and *Hotspur* and *Hostile,* both badly damaged, with *Havock,* made for the open sea. The enemy, who had barred their passage, was by now in no condition to stop them. Half an hour later they encountered a large ship coming in from the sea, which proved to be the *Ranenfels,* carrying the German reserve ammunition. She was fired upon by *Havoc* and soon exploded. The survivors of *Hardy* struggled ashore with the body of their commander, Warburton-Lee, who was awarded the Victoria Cross posthumously. He and they had left their mark on the enemy and in our naval records.

The Western Desert.

Captain Philip (Pip) Gardner of the Royal Armoured Corps won his VC at Tobruk on 23 November 1941. General Auchinleck's 'Crusader' operation had started on 18 November and certainly took the Germans by surprise; but Rommel soon counter-attacked with great force. On the evening of 22 November, 30 Corps was compelled to retire, having lost two-thirds of its tanks and leaving the garrison of Tobruk with a huge salient to defend. The situation was disturbing.

On the morning of 23 November two armoured cars of the King's Dragoon Guards had been put out of action and Captain Gardner, 4th Royal Tank Regiment, received orders to take two tanks and try to rescue them.

Captain Gardner had done some peacetime training in the Westminster Dragoons before being commissioned in the Royal Tank Regiment. He had already won the Military Cross. He had been watching the operations of the King's Dragoon Guards from his Matilda tank so that he was aware of the situation. The two armoured cars, 200 yards apart, were stationary and being pounded by enemy guns from close range.

Gardner set off at once with his two tanks and then ordered the second one to give him covering fire while he went ahead in his own. Both tanks were being hit repeatedly but the thick armour of the Matilda saved them. Gardner got his driver to manoeuvre his Matilda close to one of the cars, which was on the edge of the wire of an enemy-defended locality. He got out of his tank and tied a tow rope to the armoured car. In the process he saw an officer (Lieutenant Peter

Beames) lying beside the car with both legs blown off. Gardner lifted him into the armoured car, returned to his tank and gave the order to tow. After a few yards the tow rope was severed by a shell.

Gardner got out of his tank again and walked over to the armoured car. He decided that it was now so shattered that it was not worth recovering, but that an attempt must be made to save the wounded officer. Gardner was then hit by a shell splinter all down his left side. Nevertheless, he managed to get Beames out of the car and was carrying him on his back over to his tank when its cupula was blown off by a shell which killed his wireless operator and loader. Gardner placed Beames on the back engine louvers and climbed in alongside him to hold him in. Meanwhile his second tank had picked up the crew of the other armoured car. Both tanks then withdrew successfully in a hail of every sort of enemy projectile. Unhappily Beames did not live, but Gardner won a well deserved VC.

On 21 June 1942, when Tobruk fell to Rommel, Gardner, whose 4th Royal Tanks was almost wiped out, escaped but was captured three days later.

For twenty days, from 27 May to 15 June 1942, in Cyrenaica, Lieutenant-Colonel 'Bob' Foote, DSO, Commander of the 7th Battalion Royal Tank Regiment, Royal Armoured Corps, displayed outstanding gallantry which won him his Victoria Cross.

Churchill had been pressing Auchinleck, who had succeeded Wavell as Commander-in-Chief in the Middle East, to assume the offensive against Rommel and a mid-June attack was being considered. Rommel decided to anticipate it himself and moved into the attack on 26 May. In the next fortnight the 8th Army faced a very perilous situation resulting in the capture of Tobruk by the Germans on 21 June and a general retreat to the Egyptian frontier. Rommel considered that General Ritchie's dispersal of his armour was a major factor in the success of his own offensive.

Bob Foote, known to some of his familiars in the desert as 'Fairy Foote', was a regular officer aged thirty-seven, who had already shown great qualities of leadership and won the DSO. In the last week of May and first week of June he displayed considerable fortitude and tactical skill in two minor engagements with marauding enemy tanks.

On 13 June Foote and his tanks were ordered to delay the advance of the Panzers so that the Guards Brigade could be withdrawn that night from the Knightsbridge Box, which was in danger of being enveloped. Foote found himself engaged in a tank battle with the odds considerably in favour of the Germans, with their heavier weight of metal and longer ranging guns. For a time an opportune sandstorm, and then a smoke screen laid down by his supporting artillery, kept the Panzers back ; but they then made a more determined effort to capture the Knightsbridge Box before dark. Foote's tanks were subjected to heavy shelling from a range beyond the reach of his Matildas. His own tank was hit and badly damaged. He used his own smoke-projector cleverly to give himself cover and upset the enemy's range by keeping his tanks on the move. He moved from one tank to another to encourage them to keep firing. His only object was to hold his ground for the last hour or so of daylight, so that the Knightsbridge garrison could get away. His twenty-five Matildas, however, had been reduced to seven and it was touch and go. Largely owing to his leadership and courage they stood their ground and the garrison of the box was able to withdraw safely under cover of darkness.

When Tobruk fell on 21 June, Bob Foote led the Matildas with his usual courage. He managed to escape but was picked up and taken prisoner. Fifteen months later he escaped from his prisoner-of-war camp and rejoined the 8th Army. He has for many years been the invaluable UK Vice-Chairman of the VC and GC Association.

It was on 5 June in the Alem Hamza area further to the north that Sergeant Quentin Smythe of the 1st Royal Natal Carbineers, South African Forces, won his VC. Smythe was twenty-five years of age and came from Natal. In the early morning of 5 June his platoon, with two others of the regiment, crept forward through the minefields protecting their Alem Hamza defensive box, to carry out a surprise raid on the enemy confronting them.

At 5.20 am, while it was still dark, the South African artillery opened their barrage. At 5.30 Lieutenant K. H. Douglas, Smythe's platoon commander, gave the order to fix bayonets and the platoon closed up to the barrage. Then, with their bayonets high and shouting their Zulu war cry, they fell upon the enemy. Lieutenant Douglas was immediately wounded and Smythe ran forward to take command of the platoon. A vicious hand-to-hand encounter started with rifles, bayonets and grenades against German infantry who had taken over from the Italians. Smythe, armed only with a rifle and bayonet, killed four of them. Having captured one strongpoint Smythe led the platoon on to the next. He was hit by a grenade splinter which lodged in his head just above his right eye and afterwards he sustained three other wounds in his legs. Although he could hardly see Smythe led his men forward, but they were held up by a machine-gun about fifty yards away.

Smythe ordered his men to ground and decided he would attack the machine-gun alone with grenades. He crawled forward in the half light and then threw a grenade with the accuracy of the cricketer he was, which wiped out the whole machine-gun detachment. He then led his men forward to the final objective. Here a 47 mm anti-tank gun held them up and again Smythe went forward alone, shot two of the gunners and took the remainder prisoner.

Full daylight found him and his platoon in a dangerous salient against which the enemy concentrated their fire and began to creep round his flanks. Seeing the other platoons had withdrawn he managed to withdraw, too, with the South African artillery giving him good covering fire. In an hour and a half of stiff fighting the platoon had lost only one killed and seven wounded. They had more then achieved their task, killed a number of the enemy and returned with several prisoners.

In 1956, when I formed the VC Association, I invited Quentin Smythe to become South Africa's representative on the Committee. We have kept in the closest touch with him and he has come over to London for several of our VC and GC reunions.

22

The Three VCs and Bars.

In the whole history of the Victoria Cross only three men have won a bar to their Cross. The first one was Surgeon-Captain Arthur Martin-Leake, who won his first VC at Vlakfontein, South Africa, with the South African Constabulary on 8 February 1902, and his second as a lieutenant in the Royal Army Medical Corps, near Zonnebeke, Belgium, for his gallantry between 29 October and 8 November 1914.

Arthur Martin-Leake was born at Ware in Hertfordshire on 4 April 1874 and was thus twenty-eight when he won his first Cross and forty when he won his second. He was educated at Westminster School and University College, London, and qualified for the medical profession in 1898. When the South African War started he had just been put in charge of the District Hospital at Hemel Hempstead. As soon as the Imperial Yeomanry was formed for service in South Africa he joined the Hertfordshire Company as a trooper. He remained with them during their year's service in South Africa, taking part in several important engagements. When the Company went home Martin-Leake remained in South Africa and was employed by the Army as a civil surgeon. Later, when the South African Constabulary was formed by General Baden-Powell he joined that force with the rank of surgeon-captain.

On 8 February 1902, in a very critical engagement at Vlakfontein, he was wounded in three places when he went forward under a murderous fire to attend a badly wounded officer. Nevertheless, he remained with him to try to get him into a safer position and gave up only when completely exhausted. He was invalided back to England and was presented with his VC by King Edward VII at St James's Palace on 2 June 1902.

In 1903 Martin-Leake was posted to India as Administrative Medical Officer of the Bengal-Nagpur Railway, with its headquarters in Calcutta. In 1912-13 he contrived to see more active service with a British Red Cross unit in the Balkan War.

As soon as the First World War started in 1914 Martin-Leake obtained leave of absence from his railway in India with the idea of getting back to England and into the war at the earliest opportunity. There was a great demand for medical officers and he soon got himself appointed to the 5th Field Ambulance in the 2nd Division with the rank of lieutenant. By the time he reached his unit they were engaged in the very critical first Battle of Ypres which followed the retreat from Mons and it was there that he won the bar to his VC. During the period 20 October to 9 November he was constantly prominent in attending and rescuing wounded men left out in no-man's-land under heavy fire. His bar was presented to him by King George V at Windsor Castle on 24 July 1915.

Captain Noel Godfrey Chavasse, MC, MB, Royal Army Medical Corps, attached 1/10th Battalion Liverpool Regiment (Territorial Force), won his first VC at Guillemont, France on 9 August 1916. He was born at Oxford on 9 November 1884 and was thus thirty-two when he won his Cross. He was the son of the Bishop of Liverpool and was the twin brother of the Reverend C. M. Chavasse, MC, who was a chaplain to the Forces. Noel was educated at Magdalen College School, Liverpool College School and Trinity College Oxford. He was a fine athlete and gained a running Blue and also represented Oxford at lacrosse. He joined the RAMC in 1913 and was attached to the Liverpool Scottish. He had already been awarded a Military Cross.

During an attack he had tended the wounded in the open all day under heavy fire and during the following night. Next day he took a stretcher-bearer up to the advanced trenches and, under a murderous shell fire, carried a desperately wounded man 500 yards to safety, being wounded himself by a shell splinter in the side during the journey. Altogether he saved the lives of twenty badly wounded men, besides the ordinary cases which passed through his hands. This won him his first VC.

Within a year Captain Chavasse was awarded a posthumous bar to his vc for his gallantry (still with the 1/10th Liverpool Regiment) at Wieltje in Belgium from 31 July to 2 August 1917. Though severely wounded early in the action while carrying a wounded soldier to the dressing station he refused to leave his post and for two days not only continued to perform his duties but also went out repeatedly under heavy fire to search for and attend to the wounded who were lying out in the open. By his extraordinary energy and inspiring example he was instrumental in rescuing many wounded men who would otherwise have succumbed in the bad weather conditions. This devoted and gallant officer subsequently died of his own wounds.

Second-Lieutenant Charles Hazlett Upham won his first vc with the 20th Battalion New Zealand Military Forces at Maleme, Crete, on 22/30 May 1941 and his bar as a captain in the same battalion in the Western Desert on 14/15 July 1942.

Charles Upham was born in Christchurch, New Zealand in 1911 and was thirty years old when he won his first vc. He joined the 20th New Zealand Battalion as a private soldier in 1939 and received a commission in that battalion in November 1940. The 20th Battalion won a great reputation in Greece and Crete in 1941. Sergeant Jack Hinton won his vc in Greece in April 1941 and Sergeant Clive Hulme won his Cross in Crete immediately afterwards. In the next month, also in Crete, Charles Upham won a third vc for this very gallant New Zealand battalion.

Major Burrows, who was afterwards to command the regiment, wrote humourously in a letter to the co of the 20th Battalion, Lieutenant-Colonel Kippenberger : 'It would be a convenience if in future the names of members of the 20th Battalion who win the vc could be published in one list, and not on different days as appears to be the present practice.'

Upham went with his battalion to Greece in March 1941. They were evacuated to Crete in April and were involved in the vital operation for the defence of Maleme airfield. Charles Upham had already made a reputation as a dedicated junior leader, devoted to the interests of his men, determined that they should be well-trained and efficient and a credit to the 20th Battalion. On the other hand he had little use for spit and polish – though he fully realized that a smart appearance in times of trouble could well be a morale raiser.

The troops evacuated from Greece to Crete had nothing but their personal weapons. Guns, mortars and machine-guns were all lost. The RAF had been forced to withdraw, rather than be wiped out. The German assault on Crete was launched with all the power which they had at their disposal, overwhelming air domination by their bombers, followed by the greatest parachute landings that had ever been seen or even envisaged. In most defended areas these parachute landings were repulsed with great loss and it looked as though the airborne assault had failed. But a German force dropped to the west of the most important Maleme airfield landed without opposition and gradually began to establish itself. No attempt was made that night to restore the situation at Maleme and the Germans at once exploited this opportunity and next day started to land some big troop-carrying aircraft. The New Zealand Maoris and 20th Battalion were then ordered up to counter-attack to regain control of the airfield.

Charles Upham was still suffering from a severe attack of dysentery which he had contracted in Greece, but nothing would make him go sick. It was realized that this counter-attack must be made under cover of darkness to have any chance of success. The 20th Battalion found the Germans holding the airfield in great strength and Upham's platoon, which was leading, was soon closely engaged. Upham was an inspiration and, hurling grenades himself, accounted for a number of the enemy. Dawn was almost breaking when the forward companies of the 20th reached a position half a mile from the airfield. Upham, with his grenades and his stalwart platoon, was in the van of his company and had almost reached the edge of the airfield. With another half hour of darkness they might have made it.

Upham had taken two mortar bomb splinters in his shoulder and had his arm in a sling; he then suffered a slight wound in his foot. Enemy reinforcements were pouring into Maleme by sea and air and the 20th Battalion was driven back, with Upham still full of fight and aggression.

On 30 May the sea evacuation began from Sfakia beach. Here Upham, though suffering from his wounds, again behaved with conspicuous gallantry in attacking a force of Germans who might have interfered with the evacuation. He had certainly well deserved the first of his VCs. It was gazetted on 10 October 1941 and presented to him in

North Africa by General Sir Claude Auchinleck, who was accompanied by the New Zealand Divisional Commander, Major-General Freyberg VC.

The 20th Battalion suffered heavy casualties in the 8th Army's offensive operations of 4 November 1941 in the Western Desert. They had subsequently been brought up to strength with reinforcements. Upham had been promoted Captain and given command of C Company, with whom he had won his first VC.

On 27 May General Rommel, who had been driven out of Cyrenaica in January 1942, struck back fiercely and in the next four weeks inflicted decisive defeats on the 8th Army. The 27 June was a day of hard fighting in which, largely owing to the stubborn resistance of the New Zealanders, Rommel's 21st Panzer Division was halted. The Kiwis' 25-pounders had been most effective in withstanding the surging attack of the German tanks. On this day the New Zealand Division was holding a defensive position astride Mingar Qaim Ridge. The 20th Battalion was in the 4th Infantry Brigade, which was now commanded by Brigadier Kippenberger, who had been their battalion commander in Crete and been awarded a DSO. Colonel Burrows was in command of the 20th.

The battalion hung on to its slit trenches like grim death. Needless to say, C Company and Charles Upham continued to distinguish themselves. As the afternoon drew on to evening nowhere did the enemy break through the steady controlled fire of the New Zealanders, but they were being attacked from three sides, their artillery ammunition was down to thirty-five rounds a gun, they had no tanks and it looked as though the Germans had thrown a ring round Mingar Qaim. General Freyberg realized that they must either try to break out of this encirclement or face a complete disaster. He had barely given the preliminary orders when he was wounded. Brigadier Inglis assumed command of the division and Colonel Burrows became commander of the 4th Infantry Brigade.

The breakthrough operation was to take place half an hour before midnight. It would be done silently with the maximum of surprise. The whole division would quietly withdraw from its battle positions and assemble in darkness. The leading infantry would simply charge straight ahead and punch a hole with bullet and bayonet. Behind them the transport would be formed up waiting, with the rest of the division sitting silently in their trucks. When the assaulting infantry had made a breach, the trucks, the guns, the ambulances and the remainder of the division, would pass through the gap.

It was a gamble. It might result in a shambles ; but if it came off it could be an epic operation – which it certainly turned out to be. The Infantry of the 4th Brigade were to punch the hole – the 19th NZ Battalion leading in the centre, the 20th on the left and the Maoris on the right. Once they were through their orders were to embus and move eastwards to the Alamein defences.

Every New Zealander realized that this was to be the supreme test of his courage. It was a clear, moonlit night as the 4th Infantry Brigade assembled, leaving their slit trenches and forming up in silence on the start line, their transport tightly packed behind them. As they moved forward with their rifles held high at the ready, the only sound that could be heard was the scuffle of the men's boots in the sands and stones. It was not until they had advanced over half a mile that the first shots rang out, and then the whole of the enemy front burst into flame. No order was given but, as one man, the 4th Brigade charged forward at the double, shouting and cheering. The 19th, in the van, struck only light opposition at first but on the left the men of the 20th found themselves in a gully which was full of the enemy. Here a savage hand-to-hand battle took place with the 19th turning to help the 20th. The New Zealanders poured through the wadi, shooting, bayoneting, cheering and yelling.

At the head of C Company rushed Charles Upham, carrying a load of grenades and using them with the greatest effect. It was an eerie and a deafening scene with the chatter of machine-guns, the lines of tracer, the burning trucks, the shouts and screams and every other sound of battle.

The Germans were trying desperately to get their vehicles moving to escape from this sudden murderous assault which was engulfing them. Then the 4th Brigade were through into the open. Up went the success signal and into the gap poured the transport and the remainder of the New Zealand Division. The 20th had emerged from the cauldron thrilled but exhausted. Upham had been wounded but refused to leave his men. The 20th had suffered surprisingly few casualties. They welcomed the arrival of their trucks in which they at once embussed and moved quickly eastwards to their appointed rendezvous.

General Auchinleck wrote :

'The New Zealanders broke clean through the 21st Panzers, inflicting very serious losses on the Axis infantry in bitter hand-to-hand fighting.'

The diary of the Afrika Korps said :

'1st Battalion Panzer Grenadiers has suffered very heavy casualties as the enemy succeeded in surprising the battalion and cutting it to pieces in a hand-to-hand fight.'

At midday on 11 July the New Zealand Division, which now formed part of General 'Strafer' Gott's 13th Corps, was ordered to take part in an attack on the Ruweisat Ridge, an important feature overlooking the battlefield of Alamein. The attack was ordered to start at 11 pm on the night of 14 July, the objective being to reach the Ridge at 4.30 am on the fifteenth, when the tanks were to come forward to support them. The 4th Brigade was on the left and the 5th on the right. The 20th were in the second wave of the 4th Brigade attack.

It was pitch dark as the men spread out into formation and started to move forward. Not until they had gone three miles did they strike the first enemy posts. Then, as the fire of the defence opened on them they rushed forward at the double with fixed bayonets. It was a dog-fight with bayonets, bullets and grenades, but although some of the enemy posts fought to the last man, the Kiwis were everywhere successful.

The 20th moved forward half an hour after the assault battalions and the gap between them became wider and wider as more and more enemy posts were encountered which had escaped the attention of the leading battalions. At last the Brigade Commander became exceedingly worried and it was decided that an officer should be sent forward to find out what was happening. Charles Upham at once volunteered for this dangerous job.

Upham's jeep soon came under fire and he found that there were enemy posts in all directions which had not been dealt with. Soon he saw some enemy tanks and gave them a wide berth. At last he came across a New Zealander, Doug Green, who was acting as Forward Artillery Observer. He had lost touch with the forward battalions and was only too glad to climb aboard Upham's jeep. They came across parties of the 18th, 19th and 21st, who had lost touch with their battalions. It gradually became clear to Upham that the Ridge position, which they had thought to be the main line of resistance, was in fact only the outpost line. He returned to make his report to the brigadier, being lucky to escape capture by several parties of the enemy.

Upham had only just rejoined the 20th when they suddenly came under close fire of artillery, armoured cars and tanks. The brigade commander, Brigadier Burrows, at once ordered the 20th to go in with the bayonet. Two of Upham's C Company platoon commanders were at once killed and he was severely wounded in the left arm ; but as usual he refused to leave his company. Everything was in confusion, but soon the 20th were through and the enemy had withdrawn, leaving a large number of prisoners, both German and Italian, in the Kiwis' hands. Upham stayed on his feet until he became so weak and groggy that he had to be led away.

When the Germans counter-attacked next day with tanks much of the advantage gained by the very gallant New Zealanders' attack was lost, and Charles Upham became one of a number of officers and men of the 20th who were taken prisoner. But not before his gallantry had won him a well deserved bar to his Victoria Cross.

Charles Upham, like so many vcs from Lord Roberts onwards, was a small man, but tough as they come. Beneath a somewhat rough exterior there lurked an inner character of pure gold. To Charles a man was a man, and he respected him, or perhaps despised him, not for who he was, but for what he was. Although I was of an older generation, and seniority in itself meant nothing to Charles, we established a relationship which was of great value and pleasure, not only to ourselves, but to the very distinguished vc and gc Associations, of which I was the aged President and Charles its brightest star. And with it all he had great humility and a loathing of personal publicity. Of all the many vcs I have known and admired I would rate Charles Upham as the tops.

23

The St Nazaire Raid.

The object of this raid on 27 March 1942 was to damage the dock so badly that it would be useless – for the *Tirpitz* particularly – or indeed for any other ship. It was also a very strong U-boat base. Naturally the whole area and its approaches were heavily defended.

The plan was that the *Campbeltown*, one of the fifty old American destroyers obtained from the USA, carrying three tons of high explosives in her bows, should be driven straight at the lock gates. Other vessels were in supporting roles or carrying commandos. Commander Robert Ryder was in charge of all the naval forces; Lieutenant-Colonel Charles Newman of the Essex Regiment, was the military commander and Lieutenant-Commander Stephen Beattie was in command of *Campbeltown*.

While the main assault was in progress other landings were made at the old mole and the old entrance to the inner harbour. It was an amazing effort of navigation, planning and timing that the *Campbeltown* actually hit the dock within a few minutes of the scheduled time. From her decks Major Copeland, with a landing party, leapt ashore to destroy the dock machinery. The Germans met them with tremendous strength and furious fighting began. All but five of the landing party were killed or captured. Colonel Newman's force was to land and destroy the dock installations of the German-controlled naval base. Although Colonel Newman need not have landed himself he was one of the first ashore and led his men and directed operations personally, quite regardless of his own safety. Under his inspiring leadership the troops fought magnificently and held vastly superior forces at bay until the demolition parties had completed their work. He and his men continued fighting until finally overpowered by the enemy and taken prisoner.

Although the main objective of the expedition had been accomplished in the beaching of *Campbeltown*, Commander Ryder remained conducting operations until the last possible moment and his craft, full of dead and wounded, and subjected to an intense barrage of fire, somehow arrived safely home with the remainder of his force. Something, however, had gone wrong with the fuse of *Campbeltown* and it was not until the next day that she blew up, with a large party of German officers and technicians aboard. The lock gates were smashed and sixty enemy officers and 320 men were killed or wounded as a result of the explosion.

The British casualties from the raid were 359, of whom 144 were killed or missing and 215 taken prisoner ; 271 men returned to England. Commander Ryder was awarded the first VC for his fearless leadership throughout the operation. Lieutenant-Commander Beattie was taken prisoner and told about his VC by the Commandant of his prison camp, when it was gazetted on 25 May 1942. Colonel Newman's VC was not announced until the end of the war – on 19 June 1945.

Sergeant Thomas Frank Durrant, RE (attached to Commandos), was awarded a posthumous VC after the war on the recommendation of Colonel Newman. He had been in charge of a Lewis gun in HM Motor Launch 306. Although illuminated by enemy searchlights and wounded in many places, he continued firing until the launch was boarded and he was taken prisoner. He later died of his wounds. His gallant fight was commended by the German officer who boarded the launch.

The fifth St Nazaire VC was that of Able Seaman William Alfred Savage, who was the gun-layer of a pom-pom in a motor gunboat. Completely exposed and under heavy fire he engaged postions ashore with cool and steady accuracy and on the way out of the harbour he continued to engage attacking ships until he was killed at his gun.

24

The Battle of Wadi Akarit.

General Alexander considered this little-publicized battle on 5/6 April 1943 to have been one of the most brilliant actions of the North African Campaign and that Major-General Tuker, the architect of the victory, deserved the greatest credit for it. General Montgomery also considered it to be a brilliantly successful operation and cabled Winston Churchill to that effect – but he took all the credit himself and gave Tuker none at all. Alexander also considered that if Monty had exploited the break-in, as Tuker advised so strongly, the North African campaign could have been ended there and then.

General Rommel, who had departed before the battle took place, had previously urged, without success, that the retreating Axis army should have held Akarit (or the Gabes Gap as he called it) in preference to the very extended Mareth position, from which they had been evicted easily. The enemy were standing at Akarit and awaiting the attack of Monty's 8th Army.

The 4th Indian Division, under their brilliant commander Major-General 'Gertie' Tuker, whom both Auchinleck and Slim considered one of the best fighting commanders of the Second World War, had moved forward on the left of the 8th Army, with 51st Highland Division (Major-General Wimberley) on his right.

For the forthcoming attack Tuker had been given the most difficult task of all, the capture of the formidable Fatnassa massif, which dominated the whole very strong enemy position. Tuker had made his usual careful reconnaissance of the position before he attended the 30th Corps Commander's (General Oliver Leese's) briefing conference. The plan stipulated a mass attack all along the line in daylight, following an artillery bombardment. Tuker was convinced that such an attack would be defeated with great loss. He was of the opinion that Fatnassa must be taken first and that the Indian battalions of his 4th Indian Division, which included two battalions of Gurkhas, would be well suited to this mountainous environment and he could take Fatnassa on his own provided he was allowed to do it, with the maximum of surprise, under cover of darkness and with no artillery bombardment.

General Wimberley strongly supported Tuker and General Leese was a good enough soldier to realize the essential rightness of Tuker's plan. He consulted Montgomery, who agreed immediately. It was supposed to be the first and only time when Monty had altered one of his operation orders at the request of a subordinate commander. Tuker had quoted those lines of Adam Lindsay Gordon with regard to his undertaking:

> Look before you leap
> But if you mean leaping – don't look long
> For the weakest fence will then grow stiff
> And the stiffest doubly strong.

The 4th Indian Division, which had lost a whole brigade at Tobruk, was now only a two-brigade division. Fatnassa was no simple mountain but a labyrinthine tangle of high ridges, interlaced escarpments and twisty passages. It was the ideal ground for hillmen, who had cat's eyes in the dark, who could move silently and climb like goats. The Gurkhas would obviously be in their element and the 2nd Gurkhas (Tuker's own battalion) led the way.

The new moon had set and a slight mist clung to the earth. Several low ridges were crossed and shortly after midnight the first of the main escarpments towered ahead. In the darkness a section of cat-eyed Gurkhas detected the first enemy post. They drew their kukris and soundlessly closed in. The sentry was asleep. He never wakened. A throaty gurgle as the stroke went home, and the Gurkhas swarmed into the sangar, killing to the last man. The next two companies of the 2nd immediately pushed forward up the cliff-side through the leading company.

As the leading sections groped their way forward along the crest of the escarpment the darkness was suddenly broken by groups of dazzling flares which enemy planes hung over the mountains: they were obviously nervous. The flares were of the greatest advantage to the attackers, lighting up their final objective, which was reached successfully.

The enemy was now wide awake, acutely aware that something very unpleasant was happening but not quite knowing how, when or where. They started laying down heavy artillery and mortar concentrations on night lines and one salvo landed on the Gurkha battalion headquarters, destroying all the wireless-sets and those of the artillery observation group. For one anxious hour the commanding officer was completely out of touch with his companies. All he could hear were the sounds of a very lively battle.

The dense darkness of that boulder-studded ravine hid a great feat of arms which won a very well deserved VC for Subadar Lalbahadur Thapa of the 2nd Gurkha Rifles. Leading the two sections of his company he moved forward to secure the only pathway which led up to the escarpment at the upper end of a rocky chimney. This trail reached the top of a hill through a narrow cleft, thickly studded with enemy posts. Anti-tank guns and machine-guns covered every foot of the way, whilst across the canyon, where the cliffs rose steeply for some 200 feet, the crests were swarming with automatic gunners and mortar teams.

Subadar Lalbahadur Thapa reached the first enemy sangar without challenge. His section cut down the garrison with kukri and bayonet. Immediately every post along the twisty pathway opened fire. Straight down the ravine without pause the intrepid subadar, with no room to manoeuvre, dashed at the head of his men, through a sheet of machine-gun fire, grenades and mortar bombs. He leapt inside a machine-gun nest and killed four gunners single-handed, two with kukri and two with pistol. Man after man of his little command was killed, until only two were left. Rushing on he clambered up the last few yards of the defile through which the pathway snaked over the crest of the escarpment. Once again he flung himself single-handed on the garrison of the last sangar covering the pathway, and struck two of them dead with his kukri. This terrible Gurkha was too much for the remainder of the garrison who fled for safety screaming wildly with terror.

It is interesting to note, as illustrative of the high standards prevailing, that Colonel Showers, commanding the 1/2nd Gurkhas, had recommended the subadar only for the Military Cross. It was the Army Commander, General Montgomery, who so rightly altered the recommendation to a VC.

The Royal Sussex, advancing on the right of the 1/2nd, captured their important objective, together with 300 prisoners. The 4/16th Punjabis dashed forward, yelling their old Mussalman war cry : 'Allah ho Akbar [God is great].' When day broke every unit of the 7th Infantry Brigade had secured its objective and the 5th Infantry Brigade led by the 1/9th Gurkhas, gained their objective, taking 2000 prisoners. At 8.45 am Tuker reported to 30th Corps : 'We have bitten 6000 yards out of the enemy's position. The gate is open. Turn your armour loose.'

Monty ever cautious, and perhaps rightly so, waited until the next day before putting through General Horrock's 10th Corps *de chasse,* by which time the enemy had beaten a hasty retreat under cover of darkness. The already high reputation of the 4th Indian Division and of their commander, General Tuker, was most deservedly sky high.

25

The Dam Busters.

At this stage of the war, 1943, the only direct offensive action which could be taken against the Germans in Europe was from the air. One of the chief objectives of the bombing raids of the Allied Air Forces was the sources of Germany's war production, such as factories, oil fields and the transport system by which the weapons of war could be delivered to the troops, or to the machines, which had to use them. There were, however, other sources of power, for instance the water needed for steel production. It was this new target to which the attention of the Allies was directed.

There were three German dams in the Ruhr : the Möhne, the Eder and the Sorpe, which accounted for nearly all the water supply to that gigantic arsenal. If any, or all, of these dams could be breached in May, when the storage lakes were full, enormous floods would be caused and very serious damage to Germany's war effort would result. The dams were immensely thick and strong and it was estimated that even the heaviest type of RAF bomb then in existence would not inflict any crippling damage upon them. If, however, a bomb could be produced with sufficient penetration and explosive power, so that half a dozen of them, dropped with pin-point accuracy, could really undermine the dam and start it shifting, then a successful result might be possible.

Accordingly a team of scientists and aircraft designers, inspired by one Barnes Wallis, had for some months been working on the planning and production of such an 'earthquake bomb' which could be carried in a Lancaster aircraft. At last, towards the end of 1943, the go-ahead was given for its production. The bomb was to be seven feet in girth and of great length and could only be carried by a Lancaster bomber if the bomb doors were taken off and other alterations made. Absolute secrecy was of course essential or the already strong anti-aircraft defences of the dams would be increased and a very hazardous operation would become suicidal. The time factor was all-important.

It had been decided that a completely new RAF Squadron (Number 617) should be formed for the task, consisting of hand-picked pilots and crews. First they chose the Commander, Wing-Commander Guy Gibson, aged twenty-five, who had already made a great reputation in the RAF and won a DSO and a DFC and bar. He had joined the RAF in 1936 at the age of eighteen and took part in the first bombing attack of the war on the Kiel Canal. Soon after the Battle of Britain had begun he was transferred to Fighter Command as a night fighter pilot and during the next two months made ninety-nine sorties and shot down six enemy machines.

Gibson then returned to Bomber Command and was given command of a squadron. He achieved outstandingly successful results and his personal courage knew no bounds. He had an unusual combination of qualities, being an inspiring leader and at the same time a meticulous tactical planner. He took part in the great daylight raids on Danzig, Milan and Le Creusot and also in the 1000-bomber raid on Cologne, besides the attacks on Berlin, Gdynia, Genoa, Nuremberg and Stuttgart. Around him a team was built of his own choosing and the sixteen Lancasters were assembled at Scampton on 21 March 1943, with the necessary ground staff and equipment. Every possible priority was given to them and in a few days the new squadron personnel were all assembled – twenty-one crews, comprising 147 men, pilots, navigators, wireless operators, bomb aimers and flight engineers. Nearly all of them were under twenty-four, and nearly all of them were veterans. They were keen and eager to take part in what was obviously going to be a very special assignment. Gibson was told only that in two months' time they would have to make a low level attack in the dark, flying at sixty feet over water and that one heavy bomb would have to be dropped from each bomber within forty yards of the precise point of release. He was shown the bomb they would be using and had talks with its inventor and told roughly how it would work, bouncing along the water to the target.

From then on they practised continuously in England, Scotland and Wales, wherever stretches of water afforded the necesssary conditions. As most of the training had to be carried out in daylight the pilots were provided with synthetic screens and blue glasses to simulate the conditions of night flying. The next step was information as to their targets and the production of models of the three dams, which also showed the surrounding country. Möhne dam was 850 yards long and 140 feet thick and the lake it held back was twelve miles long and contained 140 million tons of water. Gibson was told how the bombs were to be dropped, close together so that the explosive force, plus the pressure of the water, would topple the dam over. He was also told that the attack would take place when the dams, and the moon, were full, and that these conditions would exist between 13 and 19 May.

On 15 April Gibson and his bomber crews attended a top-secret drop of prototypes of the bomb on the south coast of England. All sorts of difficulties had to be overcome before they were able to try out the strange-looking readjusted Lancasters, each fitted with a dummy of the special bomb. From time to time Bomber Command had aerial photos of the German anti-aircraft defences of the dams taken, which were carefully studied by Gibson and his chief lieutenants.

The plan was for the attack to be made in three formations. Gibson's Formation 1, approaching by the southern route, consisted of nine aircraft. They were to attack the Möhne, and after the dam had been breached, those who had not bombed would go on to the Eder. Formation 2 of five aircraft, under Flight-Lieutenant L. Munro, was to attack the Sorpe, crossing the coast by the northern route to split the German defences. Formation 3 of five aircraft, would take off two hours later and act as a reserve. The nineteen pilots of these three formations were as follows :

Formation 1

Wing Commander G. P. Gibson, DSO, DFC.
F/Lt J. V. Hopgood, DFC (missing believed killed)
F/Lt M. Martin, DFC (from Australia)
S/L M. Young, DFC (missing believed killed)
F/Lt W. Astell, DFC (missing believed killed)
F/Lt D. Maltby, DFC (missing believed killed)

S/L H. Maudsley, DFC (missing believed killed)
P/O L. Knight (from Australia)
F/Lt D. Shannon, DFC (from Australia)

Formation 2

F/Lt J. McCarthy (from USA)
F/Sgt Byers (missing believed killed)
F/Lt Barlow (missing believed killed)
P/O Rice
F/Lt L. Munrò (from New Zealand)

Formation 3

P/O Townsend
P/O Brown
F/Sgt Anderson
P/O Ottley (missing believed killed)
P/O Burpee (from Canada) (missing believed killed)

On the morning of 15 May the Air Officer Commanding informed Gibson that, provided the weather was favourable, the raid would take place the following night, 16/17 May, and that the crews could be briefed, with the strictest security precautions that afternoon. At 3 pm Gibson summoned them all and put them through an intense rehearsal lasting five hours. No one was in any doubt that the next forty-eight hours would be the most hazardous of their lives.

Next day, the sixteenth, there was a thorough checking of guns and ammunition. There followed the last hours which every first-line fighting man knows only too well, before the signal for the Off is given. At 9.10 that evening Gibson gave the signal for Munro's five aircraft of Formation 2 to start, as their route was longer. At 9.25 Gibson – his aircraft looking, as he said, like a pregnant duck with its enormous bomb – led the take-off of Formation 1.

Munro's Formation 2, having crossed the Zuyder Zee, ran into some heavy flak which destroyed his radio, without which he could neither control his formation nor even direct his own crew, and he had to turn for home. Rice's aircraft was badly hit and the bomb was lost, but miraculously he managed to fly back home. Barlow and Byers were both completely destroyed by flak.

Gibson's Formation 1 flew very low over Holland, skimming the trees and houses to avoid the flak. Astell's aircraft, however, was shot down. The remaining aircraft slipped across the Rhine but were caught in some searchlights and heavily engaged by flak and small arms fire. The rear gunners of the Lancasters replied vigorously. Gibson swung them round north of Hamm, flying as low as they dared and then, as they climbed over a ridge the Möhne lake lay before them. The moon was now well up and it was obvious that the anti-aircraft defences of the lake area, and of the dam in particular, had been alerted.

Gibson flew round the lake outside the circle of anti-aircraft defences, calling up the other aircraft of his formation, all of whom answered except Astell. Gibson then gave the signal that he was going in to attack. The Lancaster came out of the hills, speeding across the water and dropping gradually down to sixty feet. He approached the dam in a stream of flak and tracer through which it appeared impossible for anyone to remain alive. The bomb was released as they rocketed over the dam. As they looked back they saw an immense eruption of water and an enormous white column rising above the lake. Sheets of water were spilling over the dam. The raging water subsided – but the dam was still there.

Gibson signalled to Hopgood to start his attack. He was level on his run but the flak engulfed him. The bomb overshot the parapet and the bomber's tanks exploded, ripping off a wing and he spun to the ground in flames.

Gibson then ordered Mickey Martin to attack and Gibson himself led the way to take some of the flak off him. Martin's aircraft was hit several times but the bomb seemed to drop in the right place ; once again there was a tremendous explosion and a great white column rose to 1000 feet – but the dam was still there.

The fourth attack was made by Melvyn Young and again his bomb seemed to be right on target. But the dam remained, though it seemed to be wobbling.

Gibson then called on David Maltby and his bomb seemed exactly right. The air was full of mist and spray. Time was now getting short and Gibson called on Dave Shannon, but before he had started they saw that the great dam was split and crumbling and millions of tons of water were crashing down into the valley.

The crews shouted and screamed like madmen over the R/T and Gibson sent a success signal back to the Air Officer Commanding at Scampton. He told Mickey Martin and David Maltby to go home and the rest, Young, Shannon, Maudsley and Knight, to follow him to the Eder.

Meanwhile at the Sorpe, McCarthy and Brown had made several runs and dropped their bombs at the right spot. The bombs failed to break this dam, but it was not the primary target.

In the fog which was filling the valley the Eder was hard to find. Here there was no flak but the dam was surrounded by hills which made it difficult for the bombers, with their heavy bomb load, to get a run at it. Several times they tried with dummy runs but overshot it. Then Maudsley got a clear run but his bomb hit the parapet and destroyed the aircraft. Shannon tried next and seemed to have scored an accurate hit, but the dam was still standing. This left only Knight – with the last bomb. He made two runs unsuccessfully but the third time he dropped the bomb right on the spot ; the dam burst open and the vast rush of water down the valley was even greater and more spectacular than at the Möhne.

Gibson gave the signal for home. Ten out of the nineteen aircraft which had started were on their way back, but with all the German fighters alerted it was a dangerous journey. Eight of the original nineteen bombers were lost and, more important, eight crews. Out of the 133 men who had started on the mission fifty-six were missing, only three of whom escaped by parachute and became prisoners of war.

At the Operations Room in England there was great rejoicing and the news was telephoned to Sir Charles Portal, Chief of the Air Staff, who was at a conference in Washington and there were warm congratulations from the American war leaders. Guy Gibson was awarded the Victoria Cross and thirty-three of the officers and men who went with him were decorated. Later in the war, on 19 September 1944, Gibson took part in another bombing mission, from which he failed to return. Britain lost a very splendid young man whose gallant exploits will be remembered for all time.

26

Three Great Submariners.

Lieutenant-Commander Malcolm David Wanklyn, DSO, RN, of HM Submarine *Upholder* won his VC on 24 May 1941 and his achievements were an inspiration to all those submariners who followed him in the Second World War. He was resolute, relentless and imperturbable and one hundred per cent professional in his task of sinking enemy ships. In the twenty-four successful patrols which his submarine carried out in Mediterranean waters, and thirty-six attacks made, between the beginning of 1941 and April 1942 – when *Upholder* was lost – no less than twenty-three were successful.

The Wanklyn saga started early in 1941 with *Upholder* based on Malta when on his sixth patrol Wanklyn sighted a convoy of five supply ships escorted by four destroyers. He torpedoed three of the supply ships and was awarded the DSO.

Upholder continued to patrol the area and had become aware of the route the enemy used southward from Sicily. At sunset on 24 May 1941 his VC action started. At 8.30 pm he spotted three large two-funnelled transports on a south-westerly course and steaming at full speed. They were troop-carrying transports sailing for Africa. They were escorted by four or five destroyers. He had only two torpedoes left and his listening equipment was out of order. He decided to close the range and get right in among the transports to make sure of a hit.

At 8.33 he fired his torpedoes and saw a destroyer heading straight for the submarine. He immediately crash-dived and on the way down heard two explosions. He had hit the middle transport twice. Then came the inevitable depth charges which rocked the submarine dangerously. *Upholder* zig-zagged at different depths to take avoiding action.

Over thirty charges came within twenty minutes. Then four more charges exploded, but somehow they survived. Wanklyn stopped his engines and stayed silently near the bed of the Mediterranean. When they surfaced they found themselves very close to where the trooper had gone down as was evidenced by the debris and broken boats on the water. A few days later a lifeboat of the transport *Conte Rosso* was washed ashore.

Wanklyn received his vc on 11 December 1941.

Many more successful patrols were carried out and many more depth charges were survived. On 1 May 1942, Mrs Wanklyn received a letter from the Lord Commissioners of the Admiralty to say that *Upholder* was long overdue from a patrol and must be considered lost. *Upholder* had sailed from Malta on 6 April for patrol duty in the Gulf of Tripoli. On 11 April she was met by HM Submarine *Unbeaten*. After that rendezvous nothing more was ever heard of her.

Commander Anthony Cecil Capel Miers, DSO, RN, of HM Submarine *Torbay* was awarded his vc for his action in the Corfu Roads (Ionian Sea) on 5 March 1942. He was undoubtedly one of the greatest submarine commanders of all time and had a most devoted crew. In command of HM Submarine *Torbay* Miers had won a DSC and bar for his part in sinking eleven enemy ships in Mediterranean waters. *Torbay* was one of the submarines which had taken Geoffrey Keyes on his perilous journey to Rommel's headquarters, which won him the Victoria Cross.

Patrolling on the 3 March 1942 at periscope depth Miers suddenly spotted a large convoy on the horizon, escorted by three Italian destroyers. He followed them as they steamed into Corfu harbour. The destroyers went in last, protecting the other ships. Miers decided that as the sun had set and visibility was hazy he would delay his attack until the next morning.

First he had to come to the surface to recharge his batteries. Then he submerged to persiscope level and waited silently. When morning came he at once attacked three ships, two supply ships and one destroyer, firing a torpedo at each in rapid succession. He then submerged for half an hour, not knowing at the time that he had sunk the two supply ships and missed the destroyer. Then came the most hazardous moment when he had to get out of the harbour and reach the open sea. But he made it.

A few months later, on 28 July 1942, a unique occasion occurred at Buckingham Palace when Commander Anthony Miers was invested with the VC. Three of his Lieutenants received the DSO and two bars to the DSC, and twenty-four ratings received DSMs or bars to the DSM. It was the first time that officers and men of one of HM ships had all been awarded their decorations at the same investiture.

Commander John Wallace Linton, DSO, DSC, RN, of HM Submarine *Turbulent* won his VC for his many exploits between 1939 and 1943. 'Tubby' Linton was always destined for the Navy and was educated at Osborne and Dartmouth. He was a redoubtable Rugby football forward and played a number of times for the Navy between 1927 and 1930.

First of all in the submarine *Pandora* and then in *Turbulent,* Linton carried out some of the most outstanding patrols of the war. He sank one cruiser, one destroyer, one U-boat, twenty-eight supply ships – some 100,000 tons of shipping in all – and destroyed three trains by gunfire. In the last years of his life he spent 254 days at sea, submerged for nearly half that time, and his ship was hunted thirteen times and had 250 depth charges aimed at her. Like Wanklyn and Miers he combined great audacity with professional skill at his job. When back at base he was always impatient to return to the battle and he refused to be relieved of underwater duties. At last he was told that he must go home for a well-earned rest – after one more patrol. That was the one from which he never returned. On 4 May 1943 it was announced that *Turbulent* had failed to return to base and must be presumed lost. She was believed to have run into a minefield between Corsica and Sardinia. His posthumous award of the VC was made to his widow on 23 May 1943.

27

Seven Famous Bomber Pilots.

Acting Wing-Commander Hughie Idwal Edwards, DFC, won his Victoria Cross in an attack on the German port of Bremen on 4 July 1941. He was born in Western Australia on 1 August 1914 and was educated at Perth. He joined the Regular Australian Army in 1934 and was transferred to the Royal Australian Air Force in 1935 and to the RAF in 1936.

Although handicapped by a physical disability resulting from a flying accident he had repeatedly displayed outstanding gallantry in low-level attacks against strongly defended objectives. On 4 July 1941 he led his formation of bombers in a daylight attack on Bremen, one of the most heavily defended towns in Germany, only a few hours after the RAF night bombers had left the port. Edwards and his Blenheims had to go in again with all the defences alerted.

Flying at roof-top height, and passing under high-tension electric cables he finally passed through the city's powerful balloon defences. There his formation met a hail of anti-aircraft fire; but his bombs were released successfully on target though he lost four of his bombers in doing so. He then mustered and guided his remaining planes so well that he took them out of the target area without further loss. On the way back they machine-gunned emplacements, barracks and railway depots.

Hughie Edwards was the first Australian-born airman to win a VC in the Second World War and the first man in that war to win the VC, DSO, and DFC. He gained a high reputation in the RAF for leadership and discipline; the perfection of his tactics and his attention to detail contributed to his success.

On 23 August 1943 he flew on one of the memorable mass raids on Berlin. On that occasion 700 aircraft of Bomber Command attacked the enemy capital at a loss of fifty-eight bombers. They dropped 1,700 tons of high explosive on the city in less than an hour.

Hughie Edwards added a CB and an OBE to his decorations. He became Governor of Western Australia in 1974 and received a KCMG as Air Commodore Sir Hugh.

Squadron-Leader Arthur Stewart King Scarf of 62 Squadron RAF won his posthumous award of the Victoria Cross in Malaya for his attack on the Japanese Air Force base at Singora, Thailand, on 9 December 1941.

The defence of Malaya had been based on an Air Force plan by which a Japanese invasion force would be attacked at sea on the voyage from Japan. For this it had been estimated that 336 first-line aircraft would be required. In September 1940 however Japanese troops occupied the northern portion of French Indo-China which gave them a base within close striking distance of Malaya. On 16 October 1940 the commanders of the three Services in Singapore recommended that this figure of 336 should be increased to 556 first-line aircraft. But owing to the heavy losses the RAF had suffered in France and in the Battle of Britain, no additional aircraft were available for Malaya; and, when the balloon went up on 8 December 1941, General Percival, the General Officer Commanding, had only 140 second-class aircraft at his disposal. When the Japanese landed at Singora and Patani on that day they at once obtained complete air superiority over the whole area of operations – which resulted in the disastrous sinking of the two British battleships, *The Prince of Wales* and *Repulse* on 10 December.

On 9 December, the day after the landings, all available aircraft from the RAF station Butterworth in Malaya were ordered to make a daylight attack on the Japanese advanced operational base at Singora. As the aircraft detailed for the sortie, under command of Squadron-Leader Scarf, were on the point of taking off a strong force of Japanese planes dive-bombed the airfield and also made a low-level machine-gun attack. Every British aircraft was destroyed or damaged except the Blenheim piloted by Squadron-Leader Scarf, who had got his plane airborne only a few seconds before the enemy struck. He could only circle the airfield and watch the Japanese attack come and go. When the smoke cleared the extent of the disaster was revealed. Planes lay burning and corpses and wounded men were lying everywhere.

Scarf might well then have decided to abandon the operation for which his sortie had been detailed and of which he was now the only survivor. Obviously it had become a very hazardous undertaking for one plane to carry out in broad daylight. However, he decided to press on and do what damage he could to the Singora base.

The Japanese anti-aircraft defence went into furious activity as his lone Blenheim appeared and the Japanese fighters were soon up in the air. Somehow he completed his attack successfully and turned for home. Despite having been very seriously wounded he fought a brilliant evasive action in a running fight with the pursuing Japanese fighters and managed to make a successful forced landing at Alor Star without causing any injury to his crew. How he did it when so near to death was a miracle of determination and gallantry.

Scarf was rushed to Alor Star hospital, where his wife was a nursing sister, and she met the stretcher which carried him and gave two pints of her own blood. He was conscious and cheerful, but he died from secondary shock two hours after the operation.

Arthur Scarf's vc award was not gazetted until 21 June 1946.

The Japanese had gained such complete air superiority over Malaya that the small British Air Force had henceforth to confine its activities almost entirely to night operations. It soon became impossible to reinforce General Percival's force by air because the Japanese had captured the southern Burma aerodromes and cut the air route to Singapore. The projected defence plan for Malaya, therefore, was never realized.

Flight-Sergeant Rawdon Hume Middleton, 149 Squadron Royal Australian Air Force won his posthumous Victoria Cross on 29 November 1942 in an attack on the Fiat works at Turin.

He was born in New South Wales on 22 July 1916 and was a jackaroo on his father's sheep farm before joining the Air Force. He had already taken part in twenty-eight operations and this was to have been his last one before being rested. He was captain and first pilot of a Stirling bomber of 149 Squadron R A A F based at Mildenhall R A F station in East Anglia.

On the night of 29 November he was detailed as part of a force of seven aircraft to attack the Fiat Works in Turin, Italy. It was just a week since the previous attack on Turin on 20 November. They were airborne at 6.14 on that winter night, just as darkness was falling. They experienced great difficulty climbing to 12,000 feet to cross the Alps. The night was so dark that the mountain peaks were almost invisible and they had to fly high to take no chances. This led to excessive fuel consumption which was to have its effect later on. In fact it was a bad night for this long and difficult flight and only four of the seven aircraft reached their destination. Three flights were made over Turin at low level before the Fiat factory could be identified. This burned away more of their precious petrol.

By 10 pm they were ready to make their attack in face of heavy anti-aircraft fire. Middleton's aircraft was hit by a shell which burst inside the cockpit, shattered the windscreen and wounded Middleton and his second pilot, Flight-Sergeant L. A. Hyder. Middleton was hit in the head by a shell-splinter which destroyed his right eye; he was also wounded in the body and legs. Hyder received wounds in the head and both legs. The wireless operator was hit in the leg by a splinter. Middleton lost consciousness as the plane dropped down to 800 feet above Italian soil. Hyder snatched the controls just in time and raised the plane up to 1,500 feet and released the bombs. Flak poured up from the ground and scored more hits on the plane. Middleton's three gunners fired continuously until the rear turret was put out of action. The four bombers remaining left the target area with fires burning in the Fiat works. Middleton, though badly injured and in great pain, unable to speak, returned to the cockpit and took control so that Hyder could have his wounds dressed.

They faced an Alpine crossing with a damaged aircraft and insufficient fuel. They discussed abandoning the plane or landing it in northern France ; but Middleton was determined to try to reach the English coast where his crew could leave the aircraft by parachute.

Middleton's wounds worsened and as the hours went by his strength ebbed. Midnight came and after four hours they were over France where the damaged aircraft was once more engaged by anti-aircraft fire and sustained one further hit. Only the Channel stood between them and England. There was only enough fuel for a further five minutes' flying. Middleton told his crew that he would not risk hitting houses by trying to crash-land the bomber, but would put it down into the sea after the crew had baled out. He refused to countenance any argument on this decision. He flew parallel with the coast for a few miles while the crew baled out. Five of them landed safely and survived. But the front gunner, Sergeant J. E. Jeffrey, aged nineteen, of Parkstone, Dorset, and the Flight-Engineer, Sergeant J. W. Mackie of Alva, Clackmannanshire, stayed behind to assist the pilot and shared his fate when the big bomber, riddled with bullets and shell splinters and now completely out of petrol, crashed into the sea off Dymchurch. Their bodies were recovered next day. Middleton's body was recovered on 1 February at Shakespeare beach, Dover, and buried at Beck Row Cemetery, Mildenhall, on 6 February 1945. Truly, 'Greater Love hath no man than this, that he should give his life for a friend'.

Flying Officer John Alexander Cruickshank, RAFVR, won his VC on sea patrol on 17 July 1944. A Scotsman from Edinburgh he had been a member of the Territorial Regiment of the Royal Artillery for some time before the war. It was with them that he served until June 1941, when he joined the RAF. He was captain and pilot of a Catalina flying boat which was engaged on an anti-submarine patrol north-west of the Lofoten Islands. A German U-boat was spotted in the act of surfacing and Cruickshank at once attacked. He could see that the submarine was of the most modern type with a 37 mm gun and an anti-aircraft cannon. There was no indication that the U-boat had seen the Catalina which flew quite low to drop the first depth charge. Unfortunately, this jammed and Cruickshank had to turn and come in again on another run.

By this time the U-boat guns were very much in action and the Catalina was met by intense fire and repeatedly hit. The navigator and the bomber were killed and the second pilot and two other crew members wounded. But Cruickshank pressed home his attack at low level and released the depth charges himself, straddling the U-boat perfectly. There were explosions in the aeroplane, other members of the crew were hit, a fire broke out and the aircraft was filled with the fumes of exploding shells. A gunner fought the flames with an extinguisher while Cruickshank was making his attack. Cruickshank was hit in seventy-two places, receiving two serious wounds in the lungs and ten penetrating wounds in the lower limbs. The U-boat sank in a cloud of froth, smoke and oil.

147

Cruickshank collapsed and lost consciousness and the second pilot, Flight-Sergeant Jack Garnett, though wounded himself, managed to steady the plane and keep it airborne. Later Cruickshank recovered consciousness and insisted on taking over the controls. Then came the long run back to base, with Cruickshank alternating between unconsciousness and acute awareness of the ordeal being suffered by his crew. When, after several hours flying, they neared the Shetlands, he realized the difficulty of landing the shattered Catalina on the water as the second pilot was also wounded. He therefore insisted on being propped up in the second pilot's seat where he could give directions for the landing – which was made successfully.

It was a miracle that Cruickshank eventually recovered and was able to lead an active life working in the Calcutta branch of Grindlays Bank. He has kept in close touch with the Victoria Cross and George Cross Associations.

Squadron-Leader Robert Anthony Maurice Palmer, DFC, RAFVR, won a posthumous VC on 23 December 1944 when he led a formation of Lancasters to attack the marshalling yards of Cologne in daylight. But his Victoria Cross was awarded also for four years of gallant action during which he carried out 111 missions against the enemy.

His first operation was in January 1941. In the next year he took part in the first 1000-bomber raid against Cologne. He was one of the first pilots to drop a 4000 lb bomb on Germany and he could always be relied upon to press home his attack whatever the opposition. He was awarded the DFC in June 1944 and a bar on 8 December in the same year.

On Palmer's 111th and last mission it was his task as a pathfinder pilot to mark the target for the bombers which followed him. To achieve this object successfully he had to fly at a certain height, an exact air speed and on a steady course, regardless of enemy opposition.

Some minutes before Palmer reached the target he came under heavy anti-aircraft fire. Two of his engines were set on fire and there were scorching flames in the nose and bomb bay of his aircraft. Then the enemy fighters attacked in force. With his engines developing unequal power an immense effort and great determination were required to keep the damaged aircraft on a straight course. Yet he knew that if he did not do so, and complete his run-in, he would not provide an accurate and easily visible target for the following bombers. Despite everything that was hurled at him he kept a true course for the Cologne marshalling yards until they were clearly visible below him. He made a perfect approach and dropped his bombs exactly on target. His Lancaster was last seen spiralling down in flames.

So strong was the enemy ground and air opposition that half the formation failed to return. But the mission had been a priority and its success had an important bearing on subsequent ground operations.

The very gallant pilot and his crew did not die in vain, and he had packed two years of great endeavour into his short twenty-four years of life.

I now come to the best known of my seven bomber pilots of the second World War – Wing-Commander Geoffrey Leonard Cheshire, DSO, DFC. He was awarded his VC in 1944 for 'flying duties'. The end of a long official citation of his award runs as follows:

Wing-Commander Cheshire has now completed a total of a hundred missions. In four years of fighting, against the bitterest opposition, he has maintained a record of outstanding personal achievement, placing himself invariably in the forefront of the battle. What he did in the Munich operation (April 1944) was typical of the careful planning, brilliant execution and contempt for danger which has established for Wing-Commander Cheshire a reputation second to none in Bomber Command.

Leonard Cheshire was educated at the Dragon School, Oxford. He was by no means a simple character. In some ways he was a gentle person, but like so many other VC's he had a certain stubbornness in his nature which did not allow anyone to 'push him around'. The steel inside the velvet glove was well concealed but it was always there. As he grew older he seemed to develop unexpected powers of leadership until his crews would gladly follow him anywhere, feeling assured that if 'Chesh' was in charge everything would be all right. Unlike the celebrated 'Duke of Plaza Toro' he always led from the front – by example rather than by teaching or exhortation. Yet he was never a flamboyant type, neither in appearance, conduct nor character. He gave the deepest thought and careful planning to every project he undertook and yet he was quick to change the execution of a plan if circumstances demanded.

Cheshire had more influence on the progress of bombing techniques than any other airman of his generation and he was always eager to put his new thinking into operation from his place of danger in the forefront of the battle. He was, I think, the bravest of all the brave men I have been privileged to know – perhaps because he never knew the meaning of fear. He was lucky of course, as every great and successful battle leader must be.

It was while he was up at Oxford that he joined the University Air Squadron and flying became the great passion of his life. His operational career began in 1940. Against strongly defended targets he at once displayed the courage and determination of a born leader. Defying the formidable Ruhr defences he frequently released his bombs from below 2000 feet.

Over Cologne in November 1940 an anti-aircraft shell burst right inside his aircraft, blowing out one side and starting a fire. Undeterred, he went on to bomb his target and brought his plane safely home. At the end of his first operational tour in January 1941, he at once volunteered for a second. Berlin, Bremen, Cologne, Duisberg, Essen and Kiel were among the heavily defended targets he attacked.

His third operational tour started in August 1942 when he was given command of a squadron. One mission followed another until, in March 1943, he was posted to base headquarters as deputy base commander and promoted group captain. He was not at all happy there, however, and relinquished his rank at his own request in October 1943 to resume flying duties. Already he had won the DFC, DSO and two bars and was one of the most distinguished bomber pilots in the RAF.

In October 1943 Cheshire took command of 617 Squadron and opened his fourth operational tour as wing-commander. It was then that he pioneered the development of the marking system by an aircraft flying lower than the following bomber force. This method was adopted and developed in specialized raids against centres of German aircraft production. By the end of March 1944 eleven such targets had been destroyed or badly damaged, using the new marker system and a 12,000 lb bomb. Cheshire realized that the new 'master bomber' technique demanded a marker plane more manoeuvrable than the Lancaster and obtained two Mosquitoes for his low level marking task.

In April 1944 came the famous raid on Munich. Munich was selected at Cheshire's own request to test out the method of marking at low level against a heavily defended target in the heart of the Reich. The number of anti-aircraft guns in the immediate area of Munich was estimated at 200, nearly one for every aircraft in the raid. As Cheshire reached the target area he was caught in a cone of many searchlights, and as the Lancasters flying above him were dropping flares, he was illuminated from above and below. Every German gun within range opened fire on him.

Diving to 700 feet he identified the target and dropped his red-spot markers with great precision. Cheshire continued to fly over the city to assess the accuracy of the bombing and direct the operations, despite the fact that his aircraft was badly hit by shell fragments. Eventually he set course for base, still under a withering fire.

D-Day came and went and 617 Squadron was armed with the terrific new 14,000 lb bomb. On 14 June the squadron used these new bombs with great effect in an attack on the E-boat pens at Le Havre. The marker for this dangerous mission was once more Leonard Cheshire.

Finally, Cheshire was one of the only two British observers of the dropping of the atom bomb on Nagasaki.

Pilot Officer A. C. Mynarski, 419 (Royal Canadian Air Force) Squadron, Cambrai, France, 12 June 1944 won his Cross for such a very gallant act of self-sacrifice at the cost of his own life, that it is difficult to do justice to it in words.

On 12 June Pilot Officer Mynarski was the mid-upper gunner of a Lancaster aircraft detailed to attack a target at Cambrai in France. The aircraft was attacked by an enemy fighter, both port engines failed, and a fire broke out which became so fierce that the captain ordered the crew to abandon the aircraft. As Mynarski moved towards the escape hatch he saw that the rear gunner, Flying Officer George Brophy, was still in his turret and unable to leave it. The turret was in fact immoveable since the hydraulic gear had been put out of action.

Without hesitation Mynarski made his way through the flames to the rear gunner's assistance. In doing so his own parachute and his clothing, up to the waist, were set on fire. All his efforts to move the turret and free the gunner were in vain. Eventually the latter clearly indicated that nothing more could be done and that Mynarski should try to save his own life. Reluctantly, Mynarski went through the flames to the

151

escape hatch. There, as a last gesture to the trapped gunner, he turned towards him, stood to attention in his flaming clothes, and saluted before he jumped from the aircraft. His descent was spotted by the French people on the ground and they found him eventually, but so severely burned that he died.

It has often been said that many deeds of gallantry are unhonoured because no one sees them, and that is one reason why vc's are so humble about their own award. But for an amazing twist of fate and something approaching a miracle, Pilot Officer Mynarski's gallantry would never have been recorded. The Lancaster flew on, hit the ground, and as it burst asunder, Flying Officer Brophy, the trapped rear gunner, was thrown clear. In fact every one of the crew except Mynarski survived.

28

Five Gallant Canadians.

The second of the Commando raids on French ports in 1942 – the first being St Nazaire – was made against Dieppe on 19 August 1942. The Commandos played a subsidiary but important part in support of the Canadians who formed the great bulk of the attacking force. The main object of the raid was to enable the Allied planning staff to learn how best to organize the big Second Front landings in Western Europe. Dieppe served to confirm the enemy in the belief that the Allies would concentrate at the outset of the big invasion on the capture of a major port, whereas the Dieppe experiment discouraged the Allies from this idea and persuaded them to concentrate on open beaches. Whatever lessons might have been learnt from the Dieppe operation they were at a great cost in casualties, which the Canadians could never be persuaded were acceptable.

Of the 4,963 men of all ranks of the Canadian Army who embarked on the expedition, only 2,211 returned to England. Of these 589 were wounded but survived, while twenty-eight died. No less than 1,944 Canadian officers and men became prisoners of war, at least 588 of them wounded. The Canadians' total loss in fatal casualties comprised fifty-six officers and 851 other ranks, including the seven officers and sixty-four other ranks who died in captivity. Of the seven major Canadian units engaged only one brought its commanding officer back to England. Little was left of 4th Brigade, not much of the 6th. Months of hard work were required before 2nd Division became again the fine formation which had assaulted the beaches.

Three vcs were awarded for Dieppe. In addition to the two Canadians, the third was won by Captain P. A. Porteous, Royal Regiment of Artillery. The latter displayed amazing courage in activities which were far beyond the role assigned to him. He was wounded several times but he survived.

Honorary Captain John Foote, of the Canadian Chaplain Service, was regimental chaplain to the Royal Hamilton Light Infantry. Upon landing on the beach under heavy fire, he established an aid post in a slight depression. During the eight hours of continuous action he assisted the regimental medical officer in ministering to the wounded. Repeatedly he left his shelter to give first aid and carry wounded men back to the aid post. When the aid post was moved to a stranded landing craft, he continued to bring back wounded men under increasingly heavy fire and have them re-embarked. Time was limited and he was urged to embark himself, but for as long as wounded men remained behind he chose to stay to administer what comfort he could, and to go into captivity with them. His courage and calmness were quite unforgettable. The announcement of his vc was made 4 years later, on 14 February 1946.

Lieutenant-Colonel Charles Cecil Ingersoll Merritt landed his Canadian battalion of the South Saskatchawan Regiment in the face of terrific fire. From the landing point his unit's advance had to be made across a bridge which was swept by very heavy machine-gun, mortar and artillery fire; the first parties were almost completely wiped out and the bridge was thickly covered with their bodies. A daring lead was essential. Merritt rushed forward shouting, 'Come on over ! There's nothing to worry about.' He then led the survivors of at least four parties across the bridge. When they were held up once more by enemy pill boxes, Merritt again led the onslaught which succeeded in clearing them.

Although twice wounded he continued to direct the operations with great vigour. When orders for the withdrawal were issued he remained with the rear party to cover the complete withdrawal, and it was owing to his staunch defence that they all escaped. Only he was overrun by the advancing Germans and taken prisoner.

Major Paul Triquet of the Royal 22e Regiment won his Cross at Casa Berardi, Italy, on 14 December 1943. The capture of the key road junction on the main Ortona-Orsogna lateral was entirely dependent on securing the hamlet of Casa Berardi. Both this strongly defended locality and the gully in front of it had been turned by the Germans into formidable strongpoints occupied by tanks and infantry. Major Triquet's company of the Royal 22e Regiment, with the support of a squadron of a Canadian armoured regiment, was given the task of crossing the gully and capturing Casa Berardi.

Triquet's little force at once came under heavy fire from machine-guns and mortars and almost immediately all the company officers and half the men were killed or wounded. Triquet realized that if they stayed where they were they would all be wiped out. Consequently he led the remainder of his men forward to close with the enemy. In this action they destroyed four tanks and silenced several machine-guns. He took the gully and reached the outskirts of Casa Berardi. The strength of his company had been reduced to two sergeants and fifteen men. A German counter-attack, supported by tanks, started to develop almost at once.

Triquet organized his men in a defensive perimeter round his remaining tanks and he passed round the word *'ils ne passeront pas'*. He had received orders that he must hold his position at all costs, and that is what he did, repulsing repeated attacks against overwhelming odds until the remainder of the battalion relieved him next day. His force had been reduced to nine men.

Throughout the whole of this grim encounter Major Triquet showed the most magnificent courage and cheerfulness. Wherever the action was hottest he was to be seen, encouraging his men and organizing the defence. It was owing to the resolution he inspired in his handful of survivors that Casa Berardi was captured and the way opened for the attack on the vital road junction.

Major David Vivian Currie, 29th Canadian Armoured Recce Regiment, Canadian Army, won his vc at the Battle of Falaise in Normandy on 18/20 August 1944, when he was in command of a small mixed force of Canadian tanks, self-propelled anti-tank guns and infantry which was ordered to cut one of the main escape routes from the Falaise pocket. The force was held up by strong enemy resistance in the village of St Lambert sur Dives and two tanks were knocked out by 88 mm guns. Major Currie decided to enter the village alone at dusk to reconnoitre the German defences and try to extricate the crews of the disabled tanks, which he succeeded in doing despite heavy mortar fire. Early the following morning, without any previous artillery bombardment, Major Currie personally led an attack on the village in face of fierce opposition from enemy tanks, guns and infantry. By midday he had succeeded in consolidating a position half-way inside the village.

During the next thirty-six hours the Germans hurled a succession of counter-attacks against the Canadians, but each one was repulsed. At dusk on 20 August the Germans mounted an even stronger attack. But Currie's force destroyed this one almost before it was deployed. There were 300 Germans killed, 500 wounded and 2,100 captured.

Currie continued the attack and completed the capture of the whole village, thus denying an escape route to the remnants of two German armies cut off in the Falaise pocket.

Throughout three days and nights of fierce fighting, during which all the officers in his command were either killed or wounded, Major Currie's gallant conduct and contempt of danger had set a magnificent example to all ranks of the force under his command.

Major Frederick Albert Tilston, Essex Scottish Regiment, won his Cross at Hochwald Forest, near Xanten, Germany, on 1 March 1945. The 2nd Canadian Division had been given the task of breaking through the strongly fortified forest defence line which covered Xanten, the last German bastion west of the Rhine, protecting the vital Wesel bridge escape route. The Essex Scottish were ordered to breach the defences north-east of Udem and to clear the northern part of the forest through which the balance of the brigade would pass.

At 7.15 am on 1 March the attack was launched, but owing to the softness of the ground it was impractical to support the attack with tanks as had been planned. Major Tilston therefore had to keep as close as possible to the artillery barrage to get his company across 500 yards of flat open country in face of heavy machine-gun and rifle fire.

Though wounded in the head he continued to lead his men forward through a belt of barbed wire, shouting encouragement to them and using his Sten gun to great effect. He was the first to reach the enemy position and to take a prisoner. He was determined to maintain the momentum of the attack and pressed forward with his reserve platoon to the second line of enemy defences which was on the edge of the forest. He was wounded again, this time severely in the hip, but he urged his men forward and managed to rejoin them as they reached the main objective. This was an elaborate system of underground dugouts and trenches, manned in considerable strength. A grim hand-to-hand struggle ensued, with heavy casualties on both sides, and the Canadian company was reduced to twenty-six men, one quarter of its original strength.

Tilston managed to drag his pain-filled body around, moving from platoon to platoon to encourage his men to hold on. When the supply of ammunition and grenades ran desperately low Tilston crossed the bullet-swept ground to the company on his right to obtain replenishment for his troops. He made at least six of these hazardous trips and also replaced a damaged radio to re-establish contact with his battalion headquarters. He was wounded a third time, in this case in the leg, and was found lying in a bomb crater. Although very seriously wounded and barely conscious, he would not leave his company and have his wounds treated until he had given complete instructions for the defence of the captured position. He lost both his legs but survived, and his gallantry will always be remembered with pride by the Canadian Army.

29

The Italian Campaign, 1944–5.

Twenty-one VCs were awarded during the Italian campaign which saw some of the toughest fighting of the Second World War. Both Winston Churchill and his Chief of Staff, Field-Marshal Alanbrooke, complained that the Americans never appreciated the close connection which existed between the various German fronts and how much the Italian one assisted our assault on the German citadel of Europe.

Winston Churchill wrote:

As I saw the problem the campaign in Italy, in which a million or more of our British, British-controlled and Allied troops were engaged, was the faithful and indispensable comrade and counterpart to the main cross-Channel operation. I was sure that a vigorous campaign in Italy during the first half of 1944 would be the greatest help to the supreme operation of crossing the Channel on which all minds were set and all engagements made.

Field-Marshal Alexander wrote to me on 11 April 1945 from his office of Supreme Commander Allied Force Headquarters in Italy, when I was military correspondent to the Sunday Times in London:

I am always anxious that the Italian theatre of operations gets its fair share of publicity. I think the public don't always realize what a great part the soldiers out here have done in the whole strategy of the European War and that if it hadn't been for them and our victories in the Mediterranean there would have been no D-Day in Normandy. At this very moment we are fighting twenty-five German divisions, all up to their war establishments, and some of them are the best divisions in the German Army. So even if the general public don't think the Italian theatre of operations very important the Germans do.

The first VC awarded in Italy in 1944 was to Private George Mitchell of the London Scottish, who won a very gallant posthumous award of the Cross at Damiano Ridge on 20 January. The 56th Division had thrust its way across the wintry, swollen river Garigliano and onto the slopes of the main Damiano ridge where they encountered severe opposition, and Mitchell's section of the London Scottish was ordered by his platoon commander to attack some enemy machine-guns which were holding up the advance. Both the officers of the company had been wounded, and the platoon commander was killed almost as soon as he had given the order.

When a machine-gun opened fire on his company Mitchell dropped the 2-inch mortar he was carrying, seized a rifle and bayonet and charged up the hill alone. He reached the enemy machine-gun un-scathed, shot one of the crew, bayoneted another and silenced the gun. This enabled the advance to continue. A little later it was held up again by entrenched German infantry. In the face of a hail of fire Mitchell led his men forward. They captured the trench, killed six Germans and took twelve others prisoner.

Mitchell continued to lead his men forward and captured another trench. They had now reached a position just below the crest of the hill. There they were subjected to a heavy mortar attack. With their ammunition exhausted Mitchell called on his men for one more charge with the bayonet. He was the first man into the German trench where all the occupants at once surrendered. Throughout the entire operation, carried out in the dark, Mitchell had proved himself to be a tower of strength. It was a tragedy that he should have been killed when he had survived so much.

The period 6 to 10 February 1944 was one of critical importance in the Anzio beachhead. The Germans had attacked a British division with elements of six different divisions and fought a continuous series of hand-to-hand battles each one of which had its immediate effect on the position of other troops in the area and on the action as a whole. It was of supreme importance that every inch of ground should be doggedly, stubbornly and tenaciously held.

It was in these conditions that Captain (Temporary Major) William Philip Sidney of the Grenadier Guards won his Victoria Cross. He was born on 23 May 1909 and had married the elder daughter of Field-Marshal Lord Gort, vc, in 1940.

During the nights of 7 and 8 February Major Sidney was commanding the support company of his battalion. Enemy infantry attacked strongly and penetrated the position. Philip Sidney collected the crew of a 3-inch mortar firing nearby and personally led an attack with Tommy gun and hand grenade and drove them out. He then led another party in a hand-to-hand encounter. The enemy renewed its attack and a grenade struck Major Sidney in the face. Despite being weak from loss of blood and scarcely able to walk, he continued to encourage his men, with the result that the battalion's position was re-established, which had far-reaching consequences to the battle as a whole.

Major Sidney was decorated with the ribbon of the Victoria Cross by General Alexander at the Anzio beachhead on 2 April 1944. His father-in-law, who was then Governor of Malta, was present at the ceremony. Philip Sidney became Lord de L'Isle and Dudley in 1945 on the death of his father. In 1951 he became Secretary of State for Air, was created a Viscount in 1956 and became Governor of Australia in 1961.

Sepoy Kamal Ram of the 3/8th Punjab Regiment won his Cross on 12 May 1944. When the advance of his battalion had been held up by heavy machine-gun fire, whilst attempting to secure a bridgehead over the River Gari, his company commander called for a volunteer to crawl round and silence the machine-gun post. Kamal Ram volunteered at once and silenced the machine-gun by a close quarter assault. He went on to attack a second post which surrendered and, with the help of a havildar in his company, overcame a third post and enabled his company to secure a vital hold on the bridgehead.

The vc ribbon was pinned on his breast by King George vi on a hill behind the 8th Army lines near Florence on 26 July 1944. The Cross itself was presented to him by the Viceroy of India, Lord Wavell, at the Fort, Delhi on 24 October of the same year.

Kamal Ram had come to Italy in a draft. When his co had inspected the draft he had said that Kamal Ram was obviously too young and must be returned to India. Nevertheless, Kamal Ram went into action the next day and was recommended for the VC. The registration of births, marriages and deaths was not always so accurate in India as in Britain, and Kamal Ram may well have been as young as he looked. He certainly kept his youthful appearance for many years to come.

Major John Mahony, Westminster (Motor) Regiment, Canadian Army, was ordered to establish the initial bridgehead across the River Melfa at Cassino on 24 May 1944. The enemy had strong forces of tanks, self-propelled guns, and infantry in defensive positions on the east side of the river. Despite the heavy fire brought to bear on him, Major Mahony led his company across and established a small bridgehead on the other side. From 1.30 pm until 8.30 pm the company maintained itself there in face of constant enemy attack until the remaining companies of the regiment were able to cross the river to reinforce them. Major Mahony had been wounded quite early on, once in the head and twice in the leg, but he utterly refused to leave his company. The Germans had enclosed the bridgehead on three sides by an 88mm self-propelled gun to the right, a battery of four 2cm guns 100 yards to the left, a Spandau 100 yards to the left of it, a second 88mm self-propelled gun to the left of the Spandau, and about 100 riflemen with mortars and machine-guns on the left of the 88mm gun. From all these weapons Major Mahony's company was constantly under heavy fire.

Shortly after the bridgehead had been established the enemy started to show its determination to recapture it. But Major Mahony knew that the retention of the bridgehead was vital to the Canadian Corps' operation and he infused every man in his company with his own determination to retain it. It was largely owing to his heroic leadership that his company, much reduced in strength, finally drove back the German assaults, having destroyed three of their self-propelled guns and a Panther tank.

Sergeant Maurice Rogers, MM, of the Wiltshire Regiment, was awarded a posthumous VC on 3 June 1944 when acting as carrier platoon sergeant in the battalion's attack on some high ground. The leading company had taken its first objective but was then held up by strong opposition from trenches which were wired and well defended.

The carrier platoon was ordered to attack this position. They set out to do so, supported by some tanks. The platoon advanced on foot until they reached the wire which was seventy yards in front of the final objective. They had been subjected to heavy machine-gun fire, had sustained a number of casualties and the advance had come to a complete halt.

Sergeant Rogers, without hesitation, went forward by himself, firing his sub-machine gun. He cut through the wire, ran across the minefield on the other side and destroyed two of the enemy machine-gun posts. Inspired by his example the platoon followed his lead. Still alone however, and penetrating deeper into the enemy's position, he attempted to silence a third machine-gun but was blown off his feet by a grenade which burst beside him and wounded him in the leg. Undaunted, he got to his feet and continued to advance, still firing his sub-machine gun – until he was shot and killed at point-blank range. His courage and example carried his platoon forward to its final objective. Sergeant Rogers was buried in the Anzio beachhead.

Private Ernest 'Smoky' Smith was born in New Westminster, British Columbia on 3 May 1914 and was serving with the Seaforth Highlanders of Canada when he won his v c on 21 October 1944.

The 2nd Canadian Infantry Brigade had been ordered to establish a bridgehead over the Savio River and the Seaforths were selected as the spearhead of the attack. They crossed the river in most unfavourable weather and captured their objective despite heavy opposition. Torrential rain had caused the river to rise six feet in five hours, so that it was impossible to bridge to get tanks and anti-tank guns across. As the right forward company was consolidating its objective it was suddenly counter-attacked by a troop of three Panther tanks, supported by two self-propelled guns and about thirty infantrymen.

'Smoky' Smith led his Piat group of two men across an open field to the road and then managed to obtain another Piat himself. As the first enemy tanks appeared on the road, Private Smith fired at it from a range of thirty feet and put it out of action. Ten German infantrymen jumped off the back of the tank and attacked him with Schmeissers and grenades. Smith took them on with his Tommy gun, killed four of them and drove the others back. Another tank and more infantry closed in on him. Protecting a wounded comrade Smith steadfastly held his ground, knocking out another tank and two self-propelled guns. He then helped his wounded comrade to cover, obtained medical aid for him and returned to await another enemy attack.

But the Germans had had enough. No further attack developed and the Seaforths of Canada were able to consolidate the bridgehead position which was so vital for the success of the whole operation. Private 'Smoky' Smith, by his dogged determination and superb gallantry, had made it all possible.

The next vc on the Italian front, and the last one in 1944, was awarded on 9 December to Captain John Brunt, mc, of the Sherwood Foresters, who was attached to the 6th Battalion The Lincolnshire Regiment. He was twenty-two.

At dawn on the ninth the German 90th Panzer Grenadier Division counter-attacked the Lincolns' forward position in great strength with three Mark iv tanks and infantry. The house around which Brunt's platoon was dug in was destroyed. At the same time the enemy subjected the whole area to severe mortar fire. Two Sherman tanks were destroyed as were the anti-tank defences. Brunt rallied his men, moved them to another position and managed to hold the attacking infantry, though heavily outnumbered. With his Bren gun Brunt personally killed fourteen of the enemy. When his ammunition was exhausted he fired a Piat and a 2-inch mortar which he took over from casualties. His aggressive defence caused the enemy to pause and enabled Captain Brunt to reoccupy his previous position and evacuate the wounded that had been left there.

Later in the day, when a further attack developed, Brunt again displayed personal leadership of a high order. Throughout the day he was to be found where the fighting was fiercest, moving from one post to another, encouraging his men and firing any weapon which came handy. After defying death so many times during the very critical day on which he won a well deserved vc, it was tragic that he should have been killed next morning by a chance shell as he lay dozing in the sun.

In the first ten days of April 1945 four more vcs were won in Italy. The first was the posthumous award to Corporal Thomas Hunter of the Royal Marines, who was attached to 'C' Troop in the 43rd Royal Marine Commando. He was twenty-one when he met his death in winning his Cross on 2 April.

An almost unique award of the vc was that made posthumously on 8 April to Major Anders Frederick Lassen, who already held the Military Cross with two bars. The reason it was so unusual was that Major

Lassen was a Dane who, after serving in the British Merchant Service, joined the British Army when his native land was invaded by the Germans in April 1940. Major Lassen was the second Danish vc, the first being Private Thomas Dineson in France on 12 August 1918. Major 'Fred' Lassen first joined the Buffs as a private soldier and was later commissioned in the Commandos.

On the night of 8/9 April 1945 Lassen was ordered to take out a patrol of seventeen men to carry out a raid on the north shore of Lake Comacchio. His task was to cause as many casualties and as much confusion as possible, to give the impression of a major landing and to capture prisoners. He annihilated one German position with grenades and then raced forward to engage another. His patrol silenced this position but suffered several casualties. He challenged a third position but fell mortally wounded just as he had flung a grenade with such deadly effect that his patrol was able to dash in and complete its capture. Lassen refused to allow his men to evacuate him as he said it would impede their withdrawal and endanger their lives. But he had certainly more than achieved the object of his fighting patrol.

The last two vcs of the Italian campaign were won on 9 April 1945 by two very gallant Indian Army sepoys, Ali Haidar of the 6th Battalion Frontier Force Rifles and Namdeo Jadhao of the 1/5th Mahratta Light Infantry.

30

Normandy and Arnhem.

Two months after D-Day, on 6 August 1944, the British 3rd Division, under their brilliant and popular commander, Major-General 'Bolo' Whistler, were engaged in the struggle to break out of the Falaise pocket of the Normandy bridgehead, but they sustained a setback when the 10th ss Panzer Division counter-attacked at Sourdeval. Fortunately this enemy counter-stroke began just as the 1st Battalion Royal Norfolk Regiment was in process of relieving the 3rd Monmouths of 11th Armoured Division, with the result that both battalions were there together. The two battalions combined to resist this German counter-attack.

Corporal Sidney Bates, a real Cockney, had joined the Norfolks soon after Dunkirk, when he was just nineteen. His fateful hour struck when he won the vc by an act of supreme gallantry, and lost his life. The Panzer attack was heralded by a heavy and accurate artillery and mortar bombardment. Half an hour later the German assault was launched at the junction between the two forward companies of the Norfolks. Corporal Bates was commanding the right forward section of the left forward company. The enemy wedge deepened until some sixty Germans had forced their way through.

Seizing the Bren gun from the gunner, who had been killed beside him, Bates left his slit trench and charged into the enemy, firing furiously as he ran. Almost at once he fell, hit by a machine-gun burst. He dragged himself up and again advanced firing from the hip. The spread of his bullets started to have effect and the Germans began to withdraw. Bates was hit a second time much more seriously, but he staggered to his feet and tottered towards the enemy, his gun still firing.

The Germans panicked as it seemed that nothing could stop him, and some of them began to run. Bates was hit by bomb splinters and fell, mortally wounded, although still firing from a prone position. His life was ebbing away as the Germans withdrew. Corporal Bates had saved a dangerous situation single-handed and so well deserved his posthumous Victoria Cross.

The following day, 7/8 August, Captain David Jamieson won a second VC for the Royal Norfolk Regiment, on this occasion the 7th Battalion, at the River Orne. He was commanding a company which had established a bridgehead over the river, south of Grimbos. On 7 August the enemy made three counter-attacks which were repulsed by the Norfolks with heavy losses to the Germans. The last of these came at 6.30 pm, spearheaded by Tiger and Panther tanks. For four hours this assault continued, the brunt of it falling on Jamieson's company, but it was repulsed with a loss to the Germans of three tanks and an armoured car. Jamieson had exercised courage and judgement throughout.

On the morning of the eighth the enemy attacked again and a very desperate situation ensued. Two of the three tanks supporting the Norfolks were destroyed and Jamieson left his trench to direct the fire of the remaining one. He was wounded twice but refused to be evacuated as all the other officers had become casualties. He reorganized the defence and rallied his men and after several hours of bitter fighting, in which he directed the artillery support over his radio, the Germans were forced to retire, leaving a ring of dead and burnt-out tanks round Captain Jamieson's position. Through thirty-six hours of fierce fighting he had displayed outstanding qualities of leadership and courage.

The historic Battle of Arnhem saw five VC awards between 17 and 25 September 1944. The first one was to Lieutenant John Grayburn of the Parachute Regiment on the seventeenth. He was a platoon commander of the Parachute Battalion dropped ahead of the Allied armies with the task of seizing and holding the bridge over the River Rhine at Arnhem. The northern end of the bridge was captured and early on the same night Grayburn's platoon was ordered to capture the southern end which was in the hands of the enemy.

The Paras met a hail of fire from 20 mm quick-firing guns. Almost at once Grayburn was wounded in the shoulder and in the absence of any sort of cover he was obliged to withdraw.

Subsequently his platoon was ordered to capture a house vital to the defence of the bridge and, despite his wound, he led the attack which was successful. But the Germans were determined to retake it and throughout the eighteenth and nineteenth they hurled everything at it, bullets, shells and mortars. Eventually they set it on fire and Grayburn had to vacate it.

By the twentieth Grayburn's little force, still covering the approach to the bridge, were battered and exhausted but still full of fight. Enemy tanks attacked, but, still ignoring his wound, Grayburn stood his ground. He was wounded again in the back and was ordered to withdraw to the main defensive perimeter. That night he was killed, but what a gallant fight he had put up! Without his determination and fighting spirit Arnhem bridge could not have been held for those first three days.

On 19 September four more v cs were won. Captain Lionel Queripel, the 2nd Royal Sussex Regiment, who had been with his battalion in the desert, had volunteered to join the 10th Parachute Battalion after Alamein. On the afternoon of the nineteenth his company was advancing along a main road towards Arnhem when he came under heavy machine-gun fire, and he was wounded in the face. His company was reorganized and he led his men against a German strongpoint and himself killed the crew of a machine-gun and captured an anti-tank gun. Later that day he received further wounds in both arms but he continued to encourage his men to resist increasing German pressure. When they were finally forced to withdraw Queripel covered them. He fought it out to the last round he had until he was overrun and taken prisoner. He died in captivity.

Flight-Lieutenant David Lord, DFC, who won a posthumous vc on the nineteenth, was pilot and captain of a Dakota aircraft detailed to drop supplies on the afternoon of that day. British airborne troops had been surrounded and were being pressed into a small area defended by a large number of anti-aircraft guns. Air crews were warned that intense opposition would be met over the dropping zone. To ensure accuracy they were ordered to fly at 900 feet when dropping their containers.

While flying over Arnhem at 1,500 feet the starboard wing of Lord's aircraft was twice hit by anti-aircraft fire, and the starboard engine was set on fire. On learning that his crew were uninjured and that the dropping zone would be reached in three minutes, he decided to complete his mission as the troops were in dire need of supplies. He made two runs over the dropping zone and dropped his containers under heavy attack. Then, knowing that his plane must soon disintegrate, he ordered the crew to abandon the Dakota. By remaining at the controls he gave his crew a chance to escape before the aircraft fell in flames. There was in fact only one survivor and David Lord perished with his plane.

Lance-Sergeant John Baskeyfield of the 2nd Battalion South Staffordshire Regiment, serving with the 1st Air Landing Brigade of the 1st Airborne Division, was awarded a posthumous vc for his gallantry at Oosterbeek on 20 September 1944 during the battle of Arnhem, where he was in charge of a 6-pounder anti-tank gun. When the enemy developed a major attack on his sector with infantry, tanks and self-propelled guns, Baskeyfield's gun crew was responsible for the destruction of two Tiger tanks and at least one self-propelled gun. In the course of this preliminary engagement he was badly wounded in the leg and the remainder of his crew were either killed or wounded. But Lance-Sergeant Baskeyfield refused to leave his gun.

After a short interval the enemy renewed the attack with even greater ferocity. Manning his gun entirely alone, Baskeyfield continued firing until it was put out of action. Then he crawled to another 6-pounder nearby, the crew of which had all been killed, and proceeded to man it single-handed. With his second shot he scored a direct hit on a self-propelled gun, but while preparing to fire a third time he was killed. His amazing courage and spirit of aggression inspired everyone in his vicinity.

Major Robert Cain of the Royal Northumberland Fusiliers (attached to the 2nd Battalion South Staffordshire Regiment) won his Victoria Cross for his bravery throughout the whole week of 19/25 September at Arnhem. He was commanding a rifle company of the South Staffords on 19 September, which had been completely cut off from the rest of the battalion. On that day, armed with a Piat, he tackled a Tiger tank, lying in wait until the tank was close upon him. Only then did he open up with his Piat and halted the tank in its tracks. The tank swung its guns round and shot away part of a house near which he was lying. Cain was hit by machine-gun bullets and partly buried by falling masonry, but he went on firing. He scored several direct hits on the tank and immobilized it. Then he called up a 75 mm howitzer which completely disintegrated the Tiger.

Next morning, with his wounds dressed, Robert Cain was on the warpath again when three more tanks attempted to burst through the British line. Each time he held his fire with his Piat until the tank was close upon him and managed to drive it off. Despite the pain of his wounds, during the succeeding four days he was always in the forefront of the battle, refusing rest or medical attention, though his hearing was seriously impaired because of a perforated eardrum.

On 25 September the Germans made a final effort to obliterate his small force by a ferocious attack, using self-propelled guns, flame-throwers and infantry. By then all the Piats had been put out of action and Cain was armed only with a light 2-inch mortar. Yet somehow he and his Staffords hung on and his accurate mortar fire so demoralized the Germans that they withdrew in disorder. Cain's vc citation ended with the words: 'His coolness and courage under incessant fire could not have been surpassed.'

31

Midget Submarines.

The German conquest of Norway in 1940 gave them bases from which their heavy ships could menace the trade routes of the North Atlantic. When convoys to north Russia began to operate in 1941 the threat was increased. For some time the Royal Navy had been giving consideration as to how these enemy battleships and cruisers could be attacked. Their anchorages at the heads of the fiords along the Norwegian coastline were far from the open sea, out of reach of surface ships or conventional submarines, and beyond the range of the RAF heavy bombers.

Kaafjord was fifty miles up narrow channels from the open sea and well within the Arctic Circle. It was an almost land-locked basin, some four miles long by one and a half miles wide. The Germans had moored a double anti-submarine net across four-fifths of the 1000-yard wide entrance and had provided within it three widely-spaced berths for the battleships, *Tirpitz*, *Scharnhorst* and *Lutzow*, each surrounded by a triple crinoline of anti-torpedo nets. To reach the anchorage necessitated the penetration of an enemy minefield; the passage of the fiord was known to be vigilantly patrolled and guarded by gun defences and listening posts, in addition to the anti-submarine net. From aerial photographs and other information it appeared that the anti-submarine net across the entrance to Kaafjord extended from shore to shore, with a gate of some 300 feet wide at the southern end.

The X-class midget submarine was the Navy's answer to this form of defence. These midgets were shaped like a submarine but were only about fifty feet long. A single small diesel engine gave a surface speed of six and a half knots and an electric motor gave a maximum speed of four and a half knots when the midget was submerged. The battery gave a radius of over 100 miles at slow speed. The X-craft carried no torpedoes but a big load of high explosives in two large detachable charges, which were slung on either side of the hull. These charges were almost as big as the submarine itself. The method of attack was to drop these charges beneath the keel of the enemy ship where they were detonated by a clockwork fuse. The operational crew usually consisted of three officers and an engine-room artificer. The interior of the craft was nearly filled by its machinery and the space for the crew was very cramped indeed. A double-doored compartment made it possible for a diver from inside the craft to go outside when the submarine was submerged and under-way if required. There was in addition a Davis submarine escape apparatus for use in an emergency.

In the Spring of 1943 the first regular training classes began for the selected crews of the midgets. The plan for the attack on Kaafjord included six midgets: *X5*, *X6* and *X7* were to attack the *Tirpitz*; *X9* and *X10* the *Scharnhorst*. Of these, *X9*, in tow of the submarine HMS *Syrtis*, parted her tow-line unobserved at night and was never seen again. The *X8*, in tow of *Sea Nymph*, developed such defects that she had to be scuttled. The *X10* penetrated the fiord but as both her compasses and her periscope went out of action she was obliged to withdraw. So only *X5*, *X6* and *X7* remained. Lieutenant H. Henty-Creer commanded *X5*, Lieutenant Donald Cameron *X6* and Lieutenant Godfrey Place *X7*.

By September all was ready and the great adventure started. Big submarines towed the midgets to the entrance to Kaafjord and they were then slipped on 20 September. From this point *X7* and *X6* acted independently but kept fairly close together. The *X7* sighted *X5* and Godfrey Place shouted 'Good hunting and good luck.' Henty-Creer, who had been best man at his wedding seven weeks earlier, returned the greeting. The two men were never to meet again.

Stjernsund was to be negotiated submerged during the day. The X-craft dived and entered the sound. They proceeded up the sound in daylight on the twenty-first. The *X6* and *X7* spent the night of 21/22 September on the port side of the Bratt Nohn group of islands. Long before first light the *X6* got under way heading for Kaafjord, *X7* having started about an hour earlier. The first, and greatest, obstacle loomed in front of them, the submarine net at the entrance to the fiord. Somewhat precariously, they negotiated it successfully.

It was just after 5 am that the crew of *X6* saw for the first time the great ship *Tirpitz*, which had been in the forefront of their thoughts and work for the past eighteen months. She was lying with her bows pointing almost down the fiord. Slightly nearer were two tankers lying in the centre of the fiord. Some destroyers were secured alongside the bigger tanker and another destroyer was at anchor close by. The sea was glassy calm. Cameron managed to slip through the nets round the *Tirpitz* in the wake of a small coaster.

Meanwhile *X7* had run into trouble, being caught in some anti-torpedo nets. At last the midget freed herself and by 7.10 am was approaching the nets round the *Tirpitz*. Place tried to negotiate these by diving to seventy-five feet, but he was caught. Just as he began to ex-tricate himself *X6* passed through the net. After travelling for ten days and covering over 1000 miles, *X6* and *X7* arrived at their objective within a few minutes of each other.

Breakfast was being prepared in *Tirpitz*, where the crew were in blissful ignorance of what portended. Unfortunately *X6* had run aground and in freeing herself had broken surface for a few seconds. She struck a rock and surfaced again. The 2000 men aboard *Tirpitz* rushed to their battle stations, *X6* dived again and was now too close for the battleship's guns to bear, but heavy small arms fire was opened. Cameron realized that *X6* could never escape, so that he ordered all the secret equipment to be smashed. He then took the midget astern until the hydroplane guard was touching *Tirpitz*'s hull and released the two charges set to fire one hour later.

Cameron scuttled his craft and the crew baled out through the W and D compartment. As they struggled in the icy water *Tirpitz* put out a picket boat and picked them up. They were given hot coffee and schnapps which were very welcome. It was 8 am, only a quarter of an hour before the charges were timed to go off, but they had certainly not planned to be aboard the *Tirpitz* on the receiving end of their own charges.

Meanwhile, Godfrey Place had cleared the net. He steered straight for *Tirpitz* and released his charges at about 7.20 am, time-fused for one hour, just about five minutes after the *X6*'s crew had been taken aboard *Tirpitz*.

The Germans sighted *X7* for the first time although too close for any guns to bear, but the midget was peppered by machine-gun fire. The X7 again got entangled in the net and was struggling to get free when, at 8.12 am, one of the four charges went off, detonating all the others.

The explosion was shattering, the great ship heaved upward, developed a list and a huge column of water shot up into the air and fell on deck. Complete panic ensued on board *Tirpitz* and her gun crews blazed off indiscriminately, causing about 100 casualties to their own shipping in the harbour.

Place realized that X7 was now uncontrollable. He therefore took her to the surface, clambered out through the W and D, stripped off his white sweater and waved it in token of surrender. Place had ordered that the rest of the crew were to get out by the Davis escape gear. But something went wrong with it and only one escaped; the other two of the crew died at the bottom of Kaafjord.

At about 9.30 am, an hour and a half after the charges had exploded, Cameron saw the guns of *Tirpitz* fire at and apparently sink an X-craft which had appeared just outside the anti-torpedo nets, which could only have been the X5.

The *Tirpitz* had been badly damaged and it was six months before she could put to sea again. Not until the following April was she able to leave her anchorage. Six months later, she was finally bombed at anchor and sunk in a devastating air attack by twenty-one Lancaster bombers. The closing words of Sir Max Horton's signal of congratulation to the Twelfth Submarine Flotilla were:

'The long approach voyage in unparallelled conditions culminating in the successful attack on the target called for and produced the highest degree of endurance and seamanlike skill. I rejoice at the success which crowned this magnificent feat of arms'.

Both Cameron and Place were awarded the Victoria Cross.

At the end of 1944 the British Pacific Fleet, under the command of Admiral Sir Bruce Fraser, was preparing to sail to the Far East to assist the American Navy in defeating the Japanese. One of the British submarine flotillas consisted of six X-craft with their depot ship HMS *Bonaventure*. The XE craft, as the new midgets were called, were adapted to make them suitable for operating in a tropical climate.

Several other improvements had been made for increasing the explosive charge by a number of small limpet mines with magnets which would hold them to a ship's bottom. These limpet mines had to be placed by hand.

In February 1945 *Bonaventure* sailed for Australia via the Panama Canal carrying XEs *1-6*. In July 1945 they were used for two operations for which they were uniquely fitted. One was for cutting cables between Singapore and Tokyo and the other for attacking two heavy Japanese cruisers which were anchored off Singapore dockyard.

The two midgets selected for the attack on the cruisers were the *XE 1* commanded by Lieutenant J. E. Smart, RNVR, and *XE 3* commanded by Lieutenant I. E. Fraser, DSC, RNR. Operation Struggle was planned on much the same lines as the attack on *Tirpitz*. The midgets were towed by the submarines *Spark* and *Stygian* from Labuan Island, off north-west Borneo, to the entrance of Singapore Strait, a distance of about 650 miles. The Cruiser *Takao* was lying just east of the dockyard and the *Myoko* just west, near the causeway. Both cruisers were heavily armed and each carried sixteen torpedo tubes, but neither cruiser was protected by nets as *Tirpitz* had been. They were both anchored close to the shore and were partly aground at low tide. They had not been to sea for some time but their powerful guns offered considerable additional strength to the defence of the base.

The four submarines left Labuan on 26 July, travelling submerged by day and on the surface by night. The *XE 1* was in tow by *Spark* and *XE 3* by *Stygian*. Initially the operational crews of the midgets travelled aboard the towing submarines, the midgets being in charge of passage crews. After four days, in the early hours of 30 July, the operational crews took over. Then, with all four submarines submerged, the journey continued with the two midgets still in tow. Just after 11 pm that night they surfaced in the eastern approach to Singapore Strait; the tows were released and the two midgets went on alone. *Spark* and *Stygian* waited outside the eastern entrance, hoping to pick up the midgets about forty-eight hours later.

The *XE 1*, whose target was the furthest cruiser *Myoko*, went ahead, with *XE 3* following about six miles behind. Both were to operate entirely on their own. The *XE 1*, however, encountered a number of ships during the night, which seriously delayed her and resulted in her falling astern of *XE 3* and made her chances of reaching the *Myoko* negligible.

Fraser, aged twenty-three, and five foot four inches in height, in command of *XE 3,* had joined the training ship *Conway* at the age of fifteen and served with the Merchant Navy. Later he joined the RNR and was undergoing his training as a midshipman when the war started. After serving in various destroyers until 1941 he volunteered for submarines and was third officer in *Sahib* when she distinguished herself by sinking the *U 301.* He was awarded the DSC. He then volunteered for 'special and hazardous service' in 1944 and was duly appointed to X-craft. His crew consisted of First Lieutenant W. J. L. Smith, RNVR, Engine Room Artificer C. A. Read and Acting Leading Seaman J. J. Magennis. 'Kiwi' Smith had joined *XE 3* only a few weeks previously, after Sub-Lieutenant David Carey had died during a practice cable-cutting operation, probably from oxygen poisoning. But Smith was very experienced in the handling of X-craft. Read had been with *XE 3* from the beginning. Mick Magennis, the diver, was a most experienced midget submariner and had been one of *X 7*'s passage crew in the *Tirpitz* operation. He had joined the Navy as a boy and, at the beginning of the war, had served in the destroyer *Kandahar* until she had been sunk off Tripoli in December 1941. He had volunteered for submarines in 1942 and was delighted to transfer to midgets. He was twenty-five years old and ideally suited for this hazardous job being as tough as teak, as brave as a lion and a splendid swimmer.

Fraser planned to negotiate the Singapore Strait in the dark and to lie off Johore Strait just before dawn as soon as it was light enough to see the boom through his periscope.

After various adventures they had a stroke of luck on 31 July in finding the gate in the boom open and they slipped through almost alongside another vessel. Anyone looking over the ship's side could not have failed to spot the midget, but no one did. There was a lot of shipping about and the crew were becoming absolutely exhausted, avoiding the shipping and keeping the midget going with all possible speed so that they could make their attack when the tide was high.

Finally, at 12.50 pm Fraser had his first view of *Takao.* She was almost aground at bows and stern but amidships there appeared to be a deeper patch of water under her. This patch was Fraser's objective.

At 2.08 pm he turned to port and started his attack. The sea was absolutely calm and the water quite alarmingly clear. As he was approaching the cruiser he just escaped being run into by a motor-cutter crowded with Japanese soldiers going ashore. He lowered the periscope and ordered Smith to dive deep and *XE 3* grounded on the bottom. Then she rose and continued her attack. She hit the cruiser with quite a bang further forward than Fraser had intended.

After nearly an hour's manoeuvring he brought the midget to rest under the cruiser's bottom which was so encrusted with barnacles that the magnets would not hold. Magennis was out of the hatch working for well over half an hour fixing the limpet mines. He had to cut away weeds with his knife and tie the magnets in bunches of three. But he worked methodically, refusing to be hurried.

Meanwhile the rest of the crew were sweating with heat and anxiety. It was 4 pm before Magennis forced himself back in the W and D and closed the hatch. Fraser gave the order to release both side cargoes with their four tons of amatol, the clocks being set for 9.30 pm. Magennis was utterly exhausted. His hands had been torn to pieces from barnacles and it was a miracle that he was able to shut the hatch. The others gave him a drink and wrenched off his diving suit. But *XE 3* was firmly fixed below the cruiser and it looked as though they would be imprisoned there and blown up with their own explosives. It was the empty limpet container which was imprisoning them.

The situation was tense. Anyone looking over the side of the cruiser could not fail to see the craft. The limpet container had to be got clear and only a diver could do it. Magennis was almost overcome with exhaustion. The only other man with sufficient diving experience was Fraser himself; but if he failed to get back it would mean that the difficult journey home would have to be made without a navigator. Nevertheless, Fraser decided that he must go.

Magennis, feeling somewhat recovered, begged to be allowed to go himself. Reluctantly Fraser agreed. Armed with a large spanner, Magennis re-entered the W and D, swung the hatch back and left. He seemed to be gone for hours, and there were long periods of complete silence. It was a nerve-wracking ordeal for the waiting men.

At last Magennis returned to the W and D compartment. At full speed *XE 3* shot out across the banks and made for the open sea. Three hours later they reached and safely passed the boom. All the crew were utterly exhausted. They had hardly moved from their posts for twelve hours.

At 9 pm Fraser surfaced and about half an hour later they saw a great flare astern which they thought was caused by their explosives, but which was in fact an aircraft which had crashed near the dockyard and burst into flames. However, their explosives had succeeded in tearing a great hole in *Takao's* bottom, putting her completely out of action.

At 3.30 am on 1 August *XE 3* was taken in tow again by *Stygian* near Horsburgh Lighthouse. The crew of the midget had been on duty without a break and without sleep for fifty-two hours and had been submerged during the day of attack for sixteen and a half hours non-stop.

The *XE 1* was picked up by the waiting *Spark* at 10.15 pm on 1 August. They were too late to go on to the *Myoko* without risking almost certain destruction so Smart decided to attack the *Takao* and withdraw before the boom gate was shut. He was unable to get under *Takao* to place his charges accurately, but he placed them as close as he could. For this very thrilling exploit Lieutenant Smart of *XE 1* was decorated with the DSO, as was Sub-Lieutenant Smith of *XE 3*. Fraser and Magennis of *XE 3* were awarded the Victoria Cross and Artificer Read the CGM.

32

The War in Burma.

Out of the fifty-two Victoria Crosses which were won in 1944-45, twenty-seven were won on the Burma front. Unlike General Wavell, who had despised the Japanese and rated them as second-class soldiers – a fatal obsession which had resulted in inevitable retreats becoming unnecessary disasters in the earlier 1942 Burma campaign – General Bill Slim, possibly the greatest of Britain's Second World War commanders, rated the Japanese very highly indeed. In the 1942 campaign, in which Burma was lost to the currently all-conquering Japanese, Bill Slim formed his first impressions of them. He wrote later:

There can be no question of the supreme courage and hardihood of the Japanese soldiers. I know of no army that could have equalled them. They were the only troops I have ever encountered who really did fight to the last man and the last round. If you captured a position they were holding you had to kill ninety-five per cent of them – and the other five per cent killed themselves.

After the 1942 campaign was over he said:

I am never going to take on those chaps again until I have an army as well trained in jungle fighting as they are, and better equipped and supported, and an air force which can not only give me air superiority but also sufficient troop-carrying aircraft and supply planes so that the Japanese tactics of 'the hook' can be frustrated.

This is just what Bill Slim did in the two years which elapsed before his splendid Fourteenth Army shattered the Japanese and recaptured Burma in the fiercest fighting seen in the whole war.

THE WAR IN BURMA

The first VC of 1944 was awarded to Lieutenant Alec George Horwood, DCM, of the Queen's Royal Regiment on the Arakan front in Burma on 18/20 January. He had already won the DCM as a corporal at Dunkirk in 1940. As mortar officer of the Queen's he went forward to support a company of the Northamptons in their attack on a Japanese defended locality, and he repeated this action on two subsequent days. On the twentieth he led a fresh attack with great gallantry, but when he was almost through the wire and into the enemy bunker he was mortally wounded. He was buried at the Rest House, Kyauchaw and later reinterred in the War Cemetery at Imphal in Manipur.

In February and the first half of March three VCs were won in Burma, two in the Arakan and one with Wingate's raiders. Sepoy (Acting Naik) Nand Singh, 1/11th Sikh Regiment, formerly the 12th King George's Own Ferozepore Sikhs, won his VC in the Arakan on the night of 11/12 March. During the night a party of Japanese had infiltrated into the battalion positions. Nand Singh, commanding the leading section of the attack, was ordered to drive them out at all costs. He led his section up a very steep knife-edged ridge, under heavy machine-gun and rifle fire, and, although wounded in the thigh, captured the first trench at the point of the bayonet. He crawled forward alone, and although wounded again in the face and shoulder, captured the second trench by a bayonet assault. A short time later, when all his section had been killed or wounded, Naik Nand Singh dragged himself out of the trench and captured a third enemy post, killing all the occupants with his bayonet.

General Slim wrote as follows about this campaign:

The Arakan battle, judged by the size of the forces engaged was not of great magnitude, but it was nevertheless one of the historic successes of British arms. It was the turning point of the Burma campaign. For the first time a British force had met, held, and decisively defeated a major Japanese attack, and followed this up by driving the enemy out of the strongest possible natural positions that they had been preparing for months and were determined to hold at all costs. British and Indian soldiers had proved themselves, man for man, the masters of the best the Japanese could bring against them. The R A F had met and driven from the sky superior numbers of the Japanese Air Force, equipped with their latest fighters. It was a victory about which there could be no argument, and its effect, not only on the troops engaged but on the whole Fourteenth

179

Army was immense. The legend of Japanese invincibility in the jungle was smashed.

In the first ten days of April two more vcs were won in the tremendous struggle for Imphal and Kohima, which continued with relentless fury until July and was the first of two decisive battles of the South-East Asia campaign. On the morning of 6 April in the hills ten miles north of Imphal, Jemadar Abdul Hafiz of the 6th Jat Regiment, won a gallant posthumous vc when he led an assault with great dash despite having received two wounds, the second of which proved mortal. Three days later Lance-Corporal John Harman of the West Kents was killed winning his vc in a similar attack.

Lieutenant (Temporary Captain) John Niel Randle of the 1st Battalion The Royal Norfolk Regiment, won his posthumous vc on 4/6 June. He had assumed command of his company during an attack on a ridge, after the company commander had been severely wounded. Although he was wounded by a grenade, Randle displayed outstanding leadership in the capture and consolidation of the objective. He went forward and brought in all the wounded who were lying outside the perimeter.

Despite his painful wound Captain Randle refused to be evacuated and insisted on carrying out a personal reconnaissance with great daring prior to a further attack on the next Japanese position. At dawn on the following day this attack, with Randle's company leading, was almost immediately halted by a bunker sited in such a commanding position that it threatened to make the progress of the whole battalion impossible. With complete disregard for his own safety Randle attacked the machine-gun post single-handed. Although bleeding heavily from the head and mortally wounded, he reached the bunker and silenced the gun with a grenade which he hurled through the bunker slit. He flung his body across the slit so that it should be completely sealed. His self-sacrifice saved many lives and enabled his battalion to gain its objective and win a decisive victory.

His wife had a small son, whom his father had never seen. At the vc centenary reunion held in London in June 1956, Leslie Randle, then aged thirteen and a boy at the Dragon School, attended wearing his father's vc on his right breast.

Two more posthumous vc awards followed in Burma – in June to Sergeant H. V. Turner of the West Yorkshire Regiment, and Captain M. Allmand of the Indian Armoured Corps, attached to the 6th Gurkha Rifles. Then followed four awards of the Cross to Gurkhas who gained a tremendous reputation in jungle fighting as they had done in every other form of warfare. The first was to Rifleman Ganju Lama of the 1/7th Gurkha Rifles at Imphal on 12 June.

At dawn on this day a strong attack was made on this battalion by infantry and tanks, preceded by a heavy bombardment by guns and mortars. The forward Gurkha position was overrun but the battalion, well supported by an anti-tank gun and some field artillery, rallied and held on to a rear position. A counter-attack was launched to recover the lost ground by two companies of the 1/7th. In one of these went Rifleman Ganju Lama, who had already won the Military Medal and was one of the battalion's anti-tank gunners. When the counter-attack was held up by enemy tanks he crawled forward to try to get close enough to them for his gun to become effective. He managed to damage two of them and a third was knocked out by the gunners. Then he returned to his company and led a grenade attack to finish off his gallant work.

Rifleman Tulbahadur Pun of the 6th Gurkha Rifles (General Slim's battalion) won his vc on 23 June when, entirely on his own, he burst into the strongly held Japanese position known as the 'Red House', killing several of the occupants and capturing two light machine-guns and much ammunition. He then gave accurate supporting fire from the captured bunker which enabled his platoon to reach its objective.

The next two vcs were won in the third week of June by the 2nd Battalion 5th Gurkha Rifles in some very fierce fighting for two posts known as 'Water Piquet' and 'Mortar Bluff', which were situated on the hillside commanding the base at Bishenpur. These two posts were well sited and mutually supporting and their possession was essential for the protection of our communications. 'Water Piquet', the most commanding of the two posts, had been overrun by a strong force of Japanese on the night of 24/25 June.

On the afternoon of the twenty-fifth the 2/5th Gurkhas relieved 'Mortar Bluff' with a fresh garrison of forty-one men under Subadar Netrabahadur Thapa. With the loss of 'Water Piquet' the retention of

'Mortar Bluff' had become of even more vital importance. The relief was harassed by enemy snipers at close range, but was completely successful and without casualties.

A little more than an hour later, however, the enemy began to attack. Using a 75 mm and a 37 mm gun from the high ground they poured a deluge of shells into the narrow confines of the piquet. This was followed by a determined infantry attack. A fierce fight ensued in which the Gurkhas, inspired by the example set by their commander, held their ground and drove the enemy back with heavy loss.

The Japanese, when given an order had to succeed or die. Very soon they returned to the attack under cover of a night of torrential rain and inky darkness. They came forward as ferociously as before and overran two sections of the defence. The subadar, having no reserves left, went forward himself, determined that his Gurkhas should not yield another yard of ground. The struggle continued until, at 4 am, a party of eight Gurkhas with supplies of grenades and ammunition arrived as reinforcements. But it was a case of too little and too late. The Gurkhas were spotted coming up and all eight became casualties. Undismayed, Subadar Netrabahadur Thapa retrieved the ammunition himself and then counter-attacked with grenades and kukris. In the attempt he was hit in the mouth by a bullet, followed by a grenade which killed him outright. His body was found next day, kukri in hand, and a dead Japanese with a cleft skull by his side. True to the tradition of his regiment he had fought it out to the end. His was a very noble posthumous VC.

Next day a company of the 5th were ordered to recapture 'Water Piquet' and 'Mortar Bluff'. After a preliminary concentration the company went into the attack but, on reaching a false crest about eighty yards from the objective, was pinned down by heavy and accurate machine-gun fire from 'Mortar Bluff'.

Naik Agansing Rai at once led his section directly at the machine-gun under withering fire and managed to get right into the position, killing three men himself. 'Mortar Bluff' was retaken, but it was now under intense fire from 'Water Piquet', where a 37 mm gun was firing from the edge of the jungle. Agansing Rai led his section against this gun and, despite casualties, they pressed home their attack, in which the gallant naik killed three of the gun crew and his men the other two. They returned to 'Mortar Bluff' where the rest of the platoon was forming up for the final assault on 'Water Piquet'.

Once again Agansing Rai led the assault and in face of the cold fury of the Gurkhas' attack even the tough Japanese wilted and fled, and 'Water Piquet' as well was regained. But what an epic fight this three days' operation had been, against a resolute and fanatically brave enemy.

It was the 9th Gurkha Rifles who gained the next Burma vc on 9 July. Advancing alone under close-range fire Major Frank Blaker, mc, who was attached to the 9th from the Highland Light Infantry, sought out a nest of machine-guns which were holding up the attack of his battalion, and charged them single-handed. His fearless leadership, even when mortally wounded, so inspired his men that they stormed and captured the objective.

Ten more vcs were to be won in Burma in 1945 before the war ended. The first, posthumously, by Naik Sher Shah of the 7th Battalion The 16th Punjab Regiment on 19 January. The second, also posthumous, went to Lieutenant G. A. Knowland of the 1st Battalion The Norfolk Regiment. A third, posthumously, to Jemadar Parkash Singh of the 14th Battalion The 13th Frontier Force Rifles. The latter was described as not only indomitable but almost indestructable. When his platoon in a defended locality was heavily attacked he was wounded in both ankles but, propped up by his second-in-command he continued to direct operations, and when a number of his men had become casualties, he took over a Bren gun and held on until reinforcements arrived. He suffered two more wounds but in spite of intense pain and loss of blood he stayed in action, dragging himself from place to place by his hands as both his legs were useless. Although he was now obviously very near to death he shouted the Dogra warcry, which was taken up by the rest of the company. His example and leadership so inspired his men that the enemy were finally forced to retreat.

Six more vcs were awarded in the fierce fighting in Burma which took place in March 1945. They went to Naik Fazal Din of the 7/10th Baluch Regiment; Naik Gian Singh of the 4/15 Punjab Regiment; Lieutenant W. B. Weston of the Green Howards; Rifleman Bhanbhagta Gurung of the 3/2nd (King Edward VII's Own) Gurkha Rifles; Lieutenant Karamjeet Singh Judge of the 15th Punjab Regiment and Lieutenant C. Raymond, re. All but those of Gian Singh and

Bhanbhagta Gurung were posthumous awards.

The two VCs won in the capture of Meiktila were those of Naik Fazal Din and Lieutenant Weston. In an attack on a Japanese bunkered position the gallant Naik had silenced the nearest bunker with a grenade attack. He then led his section under heavy fire against the other bunker. Suddenly six Japanese, led by two officers wielding swords, rushed out. The Bren gunner shot one officer and a Japanese soldier, but was immediately attacked by the second Japanese officer, who killed him with his sword. Naik Fazal Din had at once gone to his Bren gunner's assistance but in doing so was run through the chest by the Japanese officer, the sword penetrating right through and coming out at the back. As the Japanese officer withdrew his sword, Fazal Din, despite his terrible wound, tore the sword from the hands of the officer and killed him with his own sword. He then went to the assistance of a sepoy who was struggling with another Japanese and killed the latter with his sword. Then, waving his captured sword aloft, Naik Fazal Din continued to encourage his men. He staggered to platoon headquarters to make his report and there collapsed and died.

Naik Fazal Din's gallant action so inspired his men that they continued the attack and wiped out the whole garrison of the bunker, consisting of fifty-five Japanese.

Lieutenant William Basil Weston of the Green Howards came from Ulverston in Lancashire. He was twenty-one when he' won his Cross and met his death. During his battalion's attack on the town of Meiktila on 3 March he was commanding a platoon. The task given to his company was to clear an area of the town of the enemy. From the start Weston set an inspiring example against the quite fanatical resistance of the Japanese. Each bunker position had to be dealt with separately and every Japanese had to be taken on individually. The fighting throughout the day was at close-quarters and at times hand-to-hand.

Lieutenant Weston led his platoon superbly. At 5 pm he was held up by a particularly strong position. He pressed forward into the bunker but fell desperately wounded. He realized that his men could not capture this position, nor rescue him, without heavy casualties. So he pulled the pin out of one of his greenades and blew up himself and the enemy together.

General Bill Slim writes of this fierce fighting in March as follows:

There was hand-to-hand fighting as savage as any yet experienced in a theatre where close combat was the rule rather than the exception and Japanese resistance showed no sign of breaking. They died where they fought and, as darkness fell, even in the sectors we had gained, survivors emerged from cellars and holes to renew the battle. Enemy 75 mm guns engaged our tanks and infantry at point-blank range, but they were gradually eliminated one by one until the last fifty Japanese jumped into the lake.

The capture of Meiktila in four days and the annihilation of its garrison - for as the Japanese themselves stated, hardly a man escaped - was a magnificent feat of arms. It sealed the fate of the Japanese in Burma.

On no other battle front in both world wars did any of our enemies fight with such fanatical fury and contempt for death as did the Japanese.

Bibliography

Bush, E. W., *Gallipoli* (1975)

Lucas Phillips, C. E., *Victoria Cross Battles of the Second World War* (1973)

Lummis, W., *The VC Files*

London Gazettes, The Official Citations of VC Winners

Macham, G. C., *Canada's VCs* (1956)

Merewether, J. W. B. and Smith, F., *The Indian Corps in France* (1919)

Middlebrook, M., *The First Day of the Somme* (1971)

O'Moore Creagh and Humphries, E. M., *The VC and DSO*

Slim, W., *Defeat into Victory* (1956)

Smyth, J., *The Story of the Victoria Cross* (1963)

Smyth, J., *In This Sign Conquer – The Story of the Army Chaplains* (1968)

Smyth, J., *The Valiant* (1970)

Smyth, J., *Leadership in War 1939-45* (1974)

Smyth, J., *Leadership in Battle 1914-18* (1975)

Turner, J. F., *VCs of the Royal Navy* (1956)

Turner, J. F., *VCs of the Air* (1960)

Turner, J. F., *VCs of the Army 1939-51* (1962)

War Office, *List of the Recipients of the Victoria Cross*

Index